MOCKTAILS

SEASONAL RECIPES

STEPHAN GARDNER

Disclaimer: The recipes and information provided in this book are intended for informational purposes only. The author and publisher have made every effort to ensure that the information is accurate and current at the time of publication. However, the author and publisher do not assume any responsibility or liability for errors, inaccuracies, omissions, or any outcomes related to using this information. The content of this book is not intended as a substitute for professional advice or services. Always use caution and follow proper food safety guidelines when preparing any recipes.

THE
INTRODUCTION

Dear friend,

You are holding more than just a book of mocktail recipes; it's a simple and delightful guide to the world of magical flavors and aromas. You can follow each recipe exactly as I have described; the result will always bring you joy.

What makes this collection truly unique is the opportunity it presents for you to experiment and discover. The mocktail recipes are categorized into four seasons - spring, summer, fall, and winter. Each season in nature has its distinctive essence and mood, and we may feel differently at any given moment. This approach allows you to choose a mocktail that resonates with the season or your current mood, sparking a sense of adventure and excitement in your culinary journey.

Just trust your heart - it will guide you to what you desire.

I wish for the most critical thing - may your eyes always shine with joy and pleasure.

May your positivity and smile be a reward for all your family and friends.

STEPHAN GARDNER

TABLE OF CONTENTS

Chapter 1: Spring Sensations (22 Mocktails)

TABLE OF CONTENTS

Chapter 2: Summer Delights (22 Mocktails)

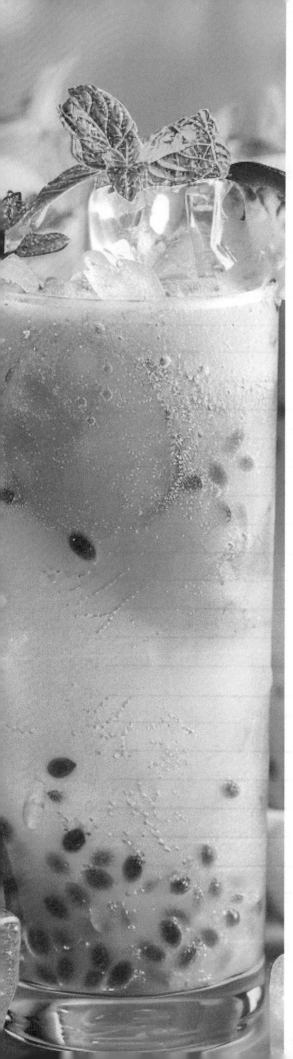

TABLE OF CONTENTS

Chapter 3: Autumn Warmers (22 Mocktails)

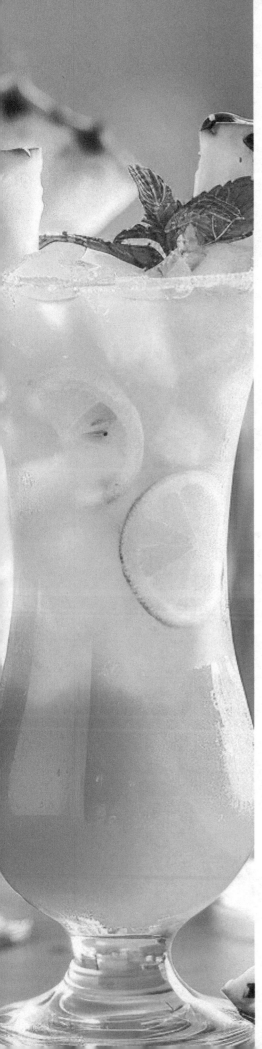

TABLE OF CONTENTS

Chapter 4: Winter Wonders (22 Mocktails)

SPRING SENSATIONS

FLORAL FIZZ

INGREDIENTS

- 1 cup fresh blueberries
- 1/2 cup fresh lemon juice (about 3-4 lemons)
- 1/4 cup honey or agave syrup (for a vegan option)
- 1/2 cup elderflower cordial
- 1 cup sparkling water
- 2 cups chilled hibiscus tea
- Ice cubes (preferably floral or regular)
- Edible flowers (for garnish)
- Fresh mint leaves (for garnish)

TOTAL TIME	CALORIES	SERVES
15 MINS	80 KCAL	4

DIRECTIONS

- Brew 2 hibiscus tea bags in 2 cups of hot water. Let it steep for 5-7 minutes, then cool and chill in the refrigerator
- Combine the strained blueberry juice, fresh lemon juice, honey or agave syrup, elderflower cordial, and chilled hibiscus tea in a large shaker. Add a few ice cubes and shake well until thoroughly mixed and chilled
- In a large shaker, combine the strained blueberry juice, fresh lemon juice, honey or agave syrup, elderflower cordial, and chilled hibiscus tea. Add a few ice cubes and shake well until thoroughly mixed and chilled
- Fill four glasses halfway with ice cubes. Divide the shaken mixture evenly among the glasses
- Top each glass with sparkling water and gently stir to combine
- Garnish each glass with edible flowers and a sprig of fresh mint for a beautiful presentation

NOTES

Sugar-Free Option: Substitute honey or agave syrup with a sugar-free sweetener such as stevia or monk fruit sweetener

MINTY MELON COOLER

TOTAL TIME	CALORIES	SERVES
15 MINS	70 KCAL	4

DIRECTIONS

- Brew 1 green tea bag in 1 cup of hot water. Let it steep for 3-5 minutes, then cool and chill in the refrigerator
- In a blender, combine the diced cantaloupe, fresh lime juice, honey or agave syrup, and fresh mint leaves. Blend until smooth
- Pour the blended mixture through a fine mesh strainer into a pitcher to remove any pulp and solids
- Add the chilled green tea to the pitcher with the strained melon mixture. Stir well to combine
- Fill four tall glasses with ice cubes
- Pour the melon mixture evenly into the prepared glasses
- Top each glass with sparkling water to add enthusiasm and volume to the mocktail
- Garnish each glass with a few melon balls, a slice of lime, and a sprig of fresh mint for a beautiful presentation

INGREDIENTS

- 2 cups diced ripe cantaloupe (or honeydew melon)
- 1/4 cup fresh lime juice (about 2-3 limes)
- 1/4 cup honey or agave syrup (for a vegan option)
- 1/2 cup fresh mint leaves, plus extra for garnish
- 1 cup sparkling water
- 1 cup chilled green tea
- Ice cubes
- Melon balls (for garnish)
- Lime slices (for garnish)

NOTES

Sugar-Free Option: Replace honey or agave syrup with a sugar-free sweetener such as stevia or monk fruit sweetener

LAVENDER LEMONADE

TOTAL TIME	CALORIES	SERVES
20 MINS	60 KCAL	4

INGREDIENTS

- 1/2 cup fresh lemon juice (about 3-4 lemons)
- 1/4 cup honey or agave syrup (for a vegan option)
- 1/4 cup dried culinary lavender
- 2 cups water
- 2 cups sparkling water
- Ice cubes
- Lemon slices (for garnish)
- Lavender sprigs (for garnish)

DIRECTIONS

- In a small saucepan, mix 1/4 cup of honey or agave syrup, 1/4 cup of dried culinary lavender, and 1 cup of water
- Bring to a boil over medium heat, stirring until the honey or agave syrup is dissolved
- Reduce the heat and let it simmer for 5 minutes
- Remove from heat and let it steep for another 10 minutes
- Strain the syrup through a fine mesh strainer into a bowl or pitcher to remove the lavender flowers. Allow the syrup to cool
- Combine the fresh lemon juice and the cooled lavender syrup in a large pitcher
- Add 1 cup of water and stir well to combine
- Fill four tall glasses with ice cubes
- Divide the lavender lemonade mixture evenly among the glasses
- Top each glass with sparkling water to add enthusiasm and volume to the mocktail
- Garnish each glass with a lemon slice and a sprig of fresh lavender for a beautiful presentation

STRAWBERRY BASIL SMASH

TOTAL TIME	CALORIES	SERVES
15 MINS	50 KCAL	4

DIRECTIONS

- In a large mixing glass or cocktail shaker, add the fresh strawberries and basil leaves
- Muddle the ingredients with a muddler or spoon until the strawberries are crushed and the basil is fragrant
- Pour in the fresh lemon juice and add the honey or agave syrup to the muddled mixture
- Add ice cubes to the shaker
- Securely close the shaker and shake vigorously for about 15-20 seconds to combine all ingredients. Chill the mixture thoroughly
- Fill four tall glasses with ice cubes
- Strain the shaken mixture equally into the prepared glasses
- Top each glass with sparkling water to add enthusiasm and volume to the mocktail
- For a beautiful presentation, garnish each glass with a lemon slice, a fresh strawberry, and a sprig of basil

INGREDIENTS

- 11 cup fresh strawberries, hulled and sliced
- 1/4 cup fresh basil leaves, plus extra for garnish
- 1/4 cup fresh lemon juice (about 2 lemons)
- 1/4 cup honey or agave syrup (for a vegan option)
- 2 cups sparkling water
- Ice cubes
- Lemon slices (for garnish)
- Fresh strawberries (for garnish)

ROSE PETAL SPRITZER

INGREDIENTS

- 1/2 cup fresh rose petals (organic, pesticide-free)
- 1/4 cup fresh lemon juice (about 2 lemons)
- 1/4 cup rose syrup
- 2 cups sparkling water
- 1 cup chilled white grape juice
- Ice cubes
- Lemon slices (for garnish)
- Fresh rose petals (for garnish)
- Fresh mint leaves (for garnish)

TOTAL TIME	CALORIES	SERVES
20 MINS	70 KCAL	4

DIRECTIONS

- In a small saucepan, combine 1/4 cup of sugar (or equivalent sweetener) with 1/4 cup of water. Bring the mixture to a boil over medium heat, stirring until the sugar is completely dissolved
- Remove the saucepan from the heat and add 1/2 cup of fresh rose petals. Let the mixture steep for 10 minutes.
- Strain the syrup through a fine mesh strainer into a bowl or pitcher to remove the rose petals. Allow the syrup to cool
- In a large pitcher, combine the fresh lemon juice with the cooled rose syrup
- Add the chilled white grape juice and stir well to combine
- Fill four tall glasses with ice cubes
- Evenly pour the rose mixture into the prepared glasses
- Top each glass with sparkling water to add enthusiasm and volume to the mocktail
- For a beautiful presentation, garnish each glass with a lemon slice, a few fresh rose petals, and a sprig of mint

GREEN APPLE REFRESHER

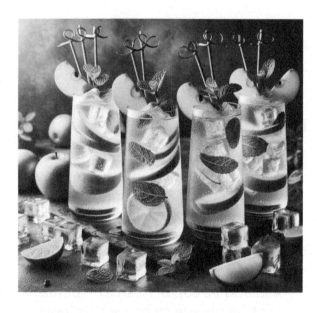

INGREDIENTS

- 2 cups green apple juice (freshly juiced or store-bought, unsweetened)

- 1/4 cup fresh lime juice (about 2 limes)

- 1/4 cup honey or agave syrup (for a vegan option)

- 1/2 cup fresh mint leaves, plus extra for garnish

- 1 cup sparkling water

- Ice cubes

- Green apple slices (for garnish)

- Lime slices (for garnish)

TOTAL TIME	CALORIES	SERVES
15 MINS	80 KCAL	4

DIRECTIONS

- If using fresh green apples, juice enough to make 2 cups. Otherwise, use store-bought, unsweetened green apple juice
- In a large mixing glass or cocktail shaker, add the fresh mint leaves
- Muddle the mint leaves using a muddler or the back of a spoon until the mint is fragrant and slightly bruised
- Add the green apple juice, fresh lime juice, and honey or agave syrup to the muddled mint leaves
- Stir or shake the mixture well to combine all the ingredients thoroughly
- Fill four tall glasses with ice cubes
- Strain the mixture equally into the prepared glasses, dividing it evenly
- Top each glass with sparkling water to add enthusiasm and volume to the mocktail
- Garnish each glass with a green apple slice, a lime slice, and a sprig of fresh mint for a beautiful presentation

CHERRY BLOSSOM DELIGHT

TOTAL TIME	CALORIES	SERVES
15 MINS	70 KCAL	4

INGREDIENTS

- 1 cup fresh cherries, pitted and halved (or 1 cup cherry juice if fresh cherries are unavailable)
- 1/4 cup fresh lemon juice (about 2 lemons)
- 1/4 cup honey or agave syrup (for a vegan option)
- 1/2 teaspoon almond extract
- 1 cup sparkling water
- Ice cubes
- Edible cherry blossoms or fresh cherries (for garnish)
- Lemon zest (for garnish)
- Mint leaves (for garnish)

DIRECTIONS

- In a large mixing glass or cocktail shaker, add the fresh cherries
- Muddle them using a muddler or the back of a spoon until the cherries are crushed and release their juices
- Pour in the fresh lemon juice and add the honey or agave syrup to the muddled cherries
- Stir until the sweetener is dissolved.
- Add the almond extract to the mixture and stir well
- Add ice cubes to the shaker
- Securely close the shaker and shake vigorously for about 15-20 seconds to combine all ingredients and chill the mixture thoroughly
- Fill four tall glasses with ice cubes.
- Strain the mixture equally into the prepared glasses
- Top each glass with sparkling water to add effervescence and volume to the mocktail
- Garnish each glass with an edible cherry blossom or a fresh cherry, a sprinkle of lemon zest, and a sprig of mint for a beautiful presentation

NOTES

- Vitamin C: 25% DV
- Calcium: 2% DV
- Iron: 1% DV

HONEYDEW MINT SPLASH

TOTAL TIME	CALORIES	SERVES
20 MINS	60 KCAL	4

DIRECTIONS

- In a blender, add the honeydew melon and cucumber cubes. Blend until smooth
- Strain the mixture through a fine mesh strainer into a bowl or pitcher to remove any pulp
- In a large mixing glass or cocktail shaker, add the fresh mint leaves
- Muddle the mint leaves using a muddler or the back of a spoon until the mint is fragrant and slightly bruised
- Add the strained honeydew and cucumber juice, fresh lime juice, and honey or agave syrup to the muddled mint leaves
- Stir or shake the mixture well to combine all the ingredients thoroughly
- Fill four tall glasses with ice cubes
- Strain the mixture equally into the prepared glasses, dividing it evenly
- Top each glass with sparkling water to add enthusiasm and volume to the mocktail
- Garnish each glass with a lime slice, cucumber slice, honeydew melon balls, and a sprig of fresh mint for a beautiful presentation

INGREDIENTS

- 2 cups honeydew melon, cubed
- 1 cup cucumber, peeled and cubed
- 1/3 cup fresh lime juice (about 3 limes)
- 1/4 cup honey or agave syrup (for a vegan option)
- 1/2 cup fresh mint leaves, plus extra for garnish
- 1 cup sparkling water
- Ice cubes
- Lime slices (for garnish)
- Cucumber slices (for garnish)
- Honeydew melon balls (for garnish)

PINEAPPLE SAGE PUNCH

TOTAL TIME	CALORIES	SERVES
15 MINS	70 KCAL	4

DIRECTIONS

- In a large mixing glass or cocktail shaker, add the fresh sage leaves
- Muddle them using a muddler or the back of a spoon until the sage is fragrant and slightly bruised
- Pour in the fresh pineapple juice and lime juice over the muddled sage leaves
- Add the honey or agave syrup to the mixture
- Stir or shake well to ensure the sweetener is fully dissolved and the flavors are well combined
- Add ice cubes to the shaker
- Securely close the shaker and shake vigorously for about 15-20 seconds to combine all ingredients and chill the mixture thoroughly
- Fill four tall glasses with ice cubes.
- Strain the mixture equally into the prepared glasses
- Top each glass with sparkling water to add enthusiasm and volume to the mocktail
- Garnish each glass with a pineapple wedge, a lime slice, and a sprig of fresh sage for a beautiful presentation

INGREDIENTS

- 2 cups fresh pineapple juice (or 1 medium pineapple, juiced)
- 1/4 cup fresh lime juice (about 2 limes)
- 1/4 cup honey or agave syrup (for a vegan option)
- 1/2 cup fresh sage leaves, plus extra for garnish
- 1 cup sparkling water
- Ice cubes
- Pineapple wedges (for garnish)
- Lime slices (for garnish)

CUCUMBER LIMEADE SMASH

TOTAL TIME	CALORIES	SERVES
15 MINS	50 KCAL	4

DIRECTIONS

- In a large mixing glass or cocktail shaker, add the cucumber cubes and fresh mint leaves
- Muddle them together using a muddler or the back of a spoon until the cucumber is crushed and the mint is fragrant
- Pour in the fresh lime juice and add the honey or agave syrup to the muddled cucumber and mint
- Add ice cubes to the shaker
- Securely close the shaker and shake vigorously for about 15-20 seconds to combine all ingredients and chill the mixture thoroughly
- Fill four tall glasses with ice cubes
- Strain the mixture equally into the prepared glasses
- Top each glass with sparkling water to add eenthusiasm and volume to the mocktail
- Garnish each glass with a lime slice, cucumber slice, and a sprig of fresh mint for a beautiful presentation

INGREDIENTS

- 1 cup cucumber, peeled and cubed
- 1/2 cup fresh lime juice (about 4-5 limes)
- 1/4 cup honey or agave syrup (for a vegan option)
- 1/2 cup fresh mint leaves, plus extra for garnish
- 1 cup sparkling water
- Ice cubes
- Lime slices (for garnish)
- Cucumber slices (for garnish)

NOTES

- Vitamin C: 20% DV
- Calcium: 2% DV
- Iron: 1% DV

RHUBARB GINGER COOLER

TOTAL TIME	CALORIES	SERVES
25 MINS	60 KCAL	4

INGREDIENTS

- 2 cups fresh rhubarb, chopped

- 1/4 cup fresh ginger, sliced

- 1/2 cup honey or agave syrup

  (for a vegan option)

- 1/2 cup fresh lime juice (about 4-5

  limes)

- 2 cups water

- 1 cup sparkling water

- Ice cubes

- Lime slices (for garnish)

- Fresh mint leaves (for garnish)

DIRECTIONS

- In a medium saucepan, combine the chopped rhubarb, sliced ginger, honey or agave syrup, and water
- Bring to a boil over medium heat, then reduce the heat and let it simmer for about 10-15 minutes until the rhubarb is soft and the mixture is slightly thickened
- Remove from heat and let it cool for 5 minutes
- Strain the syrup through a fine mesh strainer into a bowl or pitcher, pressing down on the solids to extract as much liquid as possible. Discard the solids.
- In a large pitcher, combine the rhubarb ginger syrup and fresh lime juice
- Stir thoroughly to combine
- Fill four tall glasses with ice cubes
- Divide the rhubarb-ginger mixture equally into the prepared glasses
- Top each glass with sparkling water to add enthusiasm and volume to the mocktail
- Garnish each glass with a lime slice and a sprig of fresh mint for a beautiful presentation

LEMON THYME SPARKLER

TOTAL TIME	CALORIES	SERVES
15 MINS	50 KCAL	4

INGREDIENTS

- 1/2 cup fresh lemon juice (about 3-4 lemons)
- 1/4 cup honey or agave syrup (for a vegan option)
- 1/2 cup fresh thyme leaves, plus extra sprigs for garnish
- 2 cups sparkling water
- 2 cups chilled water
- Ice cubes
- Lemon slices (for garnish)
- Thyme sprigs (for garnish)

DIRECTIONS

- In a small saucepan, combine 1/4 cup honey or agave syrup, 1/2 cup fresh thyme leaves, and 1 cup water
- Bring to a boil over medium heat, stirring until the honey or agave syrup is dissolved
- Reduce heat and let it simmer for 5 minutes
- Remove from heat and let it steep for another 10 minutes
- Strain the syrup through a fine mesh strainer into a bowl or pitcher to remove the thyme leaves. Please let the syrup cool down.
- In a large pitcher, combine the fresh lemon juice and the cooled thyme syrup
- Add 2 cups of chilled water and stir well to combine
- Fill four tall glasses with ice cubes.
- Divide the lemon thyme mixture equally into the prepared glasses
- Top each glass with sparkling water to add enthusiasm and volume to the mocktail
- Garnish each glass with a lemon slice and a sprig of fresh thyme for a beautiful presentation

KIWI MINT MOJITO

INGREDIENTS

- 4 ripe kiwis, peeled and sliced

- 1/2 cup fresh lime juice (about 4-5 limes)

- 1/4 cup honey or agave syrup (for a vegan option)

- 1/2 cup fresh mint leaves, plus extra for garnish

- 2 cups sparkling water

- Ice cubes

- Lime slices (for garnish)

- Kiwi slices (for garnish)

TOTAL TIME	CALORIES	SERVES
15 MINS	70 KCAL	4

DIRECTIONS

- In a large mixing glass or cocktail shaker, add the sliced kiwi and fresh mint leaves
- Muddle them together using a muddler or the back of a spoon until the kiwi is crushed and the mint is fragrant
- Pour in the fresh lime juice and add the honey or agave syrup to the muddled kiwi and mint
- Stir well to ensure the sweetener is fully dissolved
- Add ice cubes to the shaker
- Securely close the shaker and shake vigorously for about 15-20 seconds to combine all ingredients and chill the mixture thoroughly
- Fill four tall glasses with ice cubes
- Strain the mixture equally into the prepared glasses
- Top each glass with sparkling water to add enthusiasm and volume to the mocktail
- Garnish each glass with a lime slice, a kiwi slice, and a sprig of fresh mint for a beautiful presentation

BLUEBERRY BLISS

TOTAL TIME	CALORIES	SERVES
15 MINS	60 KCAL	4

INGREDIENTS

- 1 cup fresh blueberries
- 1/2 cup fresh lemon juice (about 3-4 lemons)
- 1/4 cup honey or agave syrup (for a vegan option)
- 1/2 cup fresh mint leaves, plus extra for garnish
- 1 cup sparkling water
- 1 cup chilled water
- Ice cubes
- Lemon slices (for garnish)
- Blueberries (for garnish)
- Mint sprigs (for garnish)

DIRECTIONS

- In a large mixing glass or cocktail shaker, add the fresh blueberries and mint leaves
- Muddle them together using a muddler or the back of a spoon until the blueberries are crushed and the mint is fragrant
- Pour in the fresh lemon juice and add the honey or agave syrup to the muddled blueberries and mint
- Stir well to ensure the sweetener is fully dissolved
- Add ice cubes to the shaker
- Securely close the shaker and shake vigorously for about 15-20 seconds to combine all ingredients and chill the mixture thoroughly
- Fill four tall glasses with ice cubes
- Strain the mixture equally into the prepared glasses
- Top each glass with sparkling water to add eenthusiasm and volume to the mocktail
- Garnish each glass with a lemon slice, a few blueberries, and a sprig of fresh mint for a beautiful presentation

NOTES

Vitamin C: 30% DV

MANGO TANGO

TOTAL TIME	CALORIES	SERVES
15 MINS	80 KCAL	4

INGREDIENTS

- 2 ripe mangoes, peeled and cubed
- 1/2 cup fresh orange juice (about 2 oranges)
- 1/4 cup fresh lime juice (about 2 limes)
- 1/4 cup honey or agave syrup (for a vegan option)
- 1/2 cup fresh mint leaves, plus extra for garnish
- 1 cup sparkling water
- Ice cubes
- Orange slices (for garnish)
- Mango slices (for garnish)
- Mint sprigs (for garnish)

DIRECTIONS

- Blend the cubed mangoes in a blender until smooth. Then, strain the mango puree through a fine mesh strainer into a bowl or a pitcher to remove any pulp
- In a large mixing glass or cocktail shaker, add the fresh mint leaves.
- Use a muddler or the back of a spoon to muddle the mint leaves until they are fragrant and slightly bruised
- Muddle the mint leaves and add the mango puree, fresh orange juice, lime juice, and honey or agave syrup
- Stir or shake well to ensure the sweetener is fully dissolved and the flavors are well combined
- Add ice cubes to the shaker, then securely close the shaker and shake vigorously for about 15-20 seconds to combine all ingredients and chill the mixture thoroughly
- Fill four tall glasses with ice cubes
- Strain the mixture equally into the prepared glasses
- Top each glass with sparkling water to add enthusiasm and volume to the mocktail
- Lastly, garnish each glass with an orange slice, a mango slice, and a sprig of fresh mint for a beautiful presentation

GARDEN PARTY PUNCH

TOTAL TIME	CALORIES	SERVES
20 MINS	50 KCAL	4

INGREDIENTS

- 1 cup fresh strawberries, hulled and sliced
- 1/2 cup fresh cucumber, peeled and sliced
- 1/2 cup fresh orange juice (about 4 oranges)
- 1/4 cup fresh lemon juice (about 4 lemons)
- 1/4 cup honey or agave syrup (for a vegan option)
- 1/2 cup fresh mint leaves, plus extra for garnish
- 2 cups sparkling water
- Ice cubes
- Orange slices (for garnish)
- Cucumber slices (for garnish)
- Mint sprigs (for garnish)

DIRECTIONS

- Add fresh strawberries, cucumber slices, and mint leaves to a large mixing bowl or pitcher
- Muddle the ingredients together using a muddler or the back of a spoon until the fruits are crushed and the mint is fragrant
- Pour in the fresh orange juice and lemon juice over the muddled mixture
- Add honey or agave syrup to the mixture
- Stir well to ensure the sweetener is fully dissolved and the flavors are well combined
- Add ice cubes to the mixture to chill it thoroughly
- Fill eight tall glasses with ice cubes
- Divide the mixture equally into the prepared glasses
- Top each glass with sparkling water to add enthusiasm and volume to the mocktail
- For a beautiful presentation, garnish each glass with an orange slice, a cucumber slice, and a sprig of fresh mint

GRAPEFRUIT ROSEMARY FIZZ

TOTAL TIME	CALORIES	SERVES
15 MINS	60 KCAL	4

INGREDIENTS

- 2 cups fresh grapefruit juice (about 2-3 grapefruits)
- 1/4 cup fresh lemon juice (about 2 lemons)
- 1/4 cup honey or agave syrup (for a vegan option)
- 2 sprigs fresh rosemary, plus extra for garnish
- 2 cups sparkling water
- Ice cubes
- Grapefruit slices (for garnish)
- Lemon zest (for garnish)

DIRECTIONS

- In a small saucepan, combine 1/4 cup of honey or agave syrup, 1/2 cup of water, and some sprigs of rosemary
- Bring the mixture to a boil over medium heat, stirring until the sweetener is completely dissolved
- Reduce the heat and let the mixture simmer for 5 minutes
- Remove the saucepan from the heat and let the mixture steep for an additional 10 minutes
- Strain the syrup through a fine mesh strainer into a bowl or pitcher to remove the rosemary leaves and allow the syrup to cool
- In a large pitcher, combine the fresh grapefruit juice, lemon juice, and the cooled rosemary syrup. Stir well to combine
- Fill four tall glasses with ice cubes
- Divide the grapefruit-rosemary mixture equally into the prepared glasses
- Top each glass with sparkling water to add enthusiasm and volume to the mocktail
- Garnish each glass with a grapefruit slice, a sprig of fresh rosemary, and a sprinkle of lemon zest for a beautiful presentation

PEACH BELLINI MOCKTAIL

INGREDIENTS

- 2 ripe peaches, peeled and sliced

- 1/4 cup fresh lemon juice (about 2 lemons)

- 1/4 cup honey or agave syrup (for a vegan option)

- 2 cups sparkling water or club soda

- Ice cubes

- Peach slices (for garnish)

- Mint leaves (for garnish)

TOTAL TIME	CALORIES	SERVES
15 MINS	50 KCAL	4

DIRECTIONS

- In a blender, add the peeled and sliced peaches. Blend until smooth. Strain the peach puree through a fine mesh strainer into a bowl or pitcher to remove any pulp
- In a large pitcher, combine the fresh lemon juice, honey or agave syrup, and the strained peach puree. Stir well to ensure the sweetener is fully dissolved and the flavors are well combined
- Add ice cubes to a cocktail shaker, pour in the peach mixture, and shake vigorously for about 15-20 seconds to combine all ingredients and chill the mixture thoroughly
- Fill four champagne flutes or tall glasses with ice cubes
- Strain the mixture equally into the prepared glasses
- Top each glass with sparkling water or club soda to add enthusiasm and volume to the mocktail
- Garnish each glass with a peach slice and a sprig of fresh mint for a beautiful presentation

NOTES
Freeze small mint leaves or lemon zest in ice cubes to add a decorative and flavorful touch to your mocktail.

HIBISCUS COOLER

TOTAL TIME	CALORIES	SERVES
15 MINS	50 KCAL	4

DIRECTIONS

- Bring 2 cups of water to a boil. Remove from heat and add the hibiscus tea bags
- Let it steep for 5-7 minutes. Remove the tea bags and allow the tea to cool to room temperature
- In a large pitcher, combine the cooled hibiscus tea, fresh lime juice, and honey or agave syrup
- Stir well to ensure the sweetener is fully dissolved and the flavors are well combined
- Add ice cubes to the pitcher to chill the mixture thoroughly
- Fill four tall glasses with ice cubes
- Divide the hibiscus mixture equally into the prepared glasses
- Top each glass with sparkling water to add enthusiasm and volume to the mocktail
- Garnish each glass with a lime slice, a sprig of fresh mint, and edible flowers for a beautiful presentation

INGREDIENTS

- 2 cups water
- 4 hibiscus tea bags
- 1/4 cup fresh lime juice (about 2-3 limes)
- 1/4 cup honey or agave syrup (for a vegan option)
- 1 cup sparkling water
- Ice cubes
- Lime slices (for garnish)
- Mint leaves (for garnish)
- Edible flowers (for garnish, optional)

NOTES

Sugar-Free Option: Substitute honey or agave syrup with a sugar-free sweetener such as stevia or monk fruit sweetener

APRICOT DELIGHT

TOTAL TIME	CALORIES	SERVES
15 MINS	60 KCAL	4

INGREDIENTS

- 1 cup fresh apricots, pitted and chopped (or 1 cup apricot nectar)
- 1/4 cup fresh lemon juice (about 2 lemons)
- 1/4 cup honey or agave syrup (for a vegan option)
- 1/2 cup fresh mint leaves, plus extra for garnish
- 1 cup sparkling water
- 1 cup chilled water
- Ice cubes
- Lemon slices (for garnish)
- Mint sprigs (for garnish)

DIRECTIONS

- Add the chopped apricots to a blender and blend until smooth. Strain the apricot puree through a fine mesh strainer into a bowl or pitcher to remove any pulp
- In a large mixing glass or cocktail shaker, add the fresh mint leaves
- Muddle the mint leaves using a muddler or the back of a spoon until the mint is fragrant and slightly bruised
- Add the apricot puree, fresh lemon juice, and honey or agave syrup to the muddled mint leaves
- Stir well to ensure the sweetener is fully dissolved and the flavors are well combined
- Add ice cubes to the shaker
- Securely close the shaker and shake vigorously for about 15-20 seconds to combine all ingredients and chill the mixture thoroughly
- Fill four tall glasses with ice cubes
- Strain the mixture equally into the prepared glasses
- Top each glass with sparkling water to add enthusiasm and volume to the mocktail
- Garnish each glass with a lemon slice and a sprig of fresh mint for a beautiful presentation

STRAWBERRY BOOM

TOTAL TIME	CALORIES	SERVES
15 MINS	**60 KCAL**	**4**

DIRECTIONS

- In a large mixing glass or cocktail shaker, add the sliced strawberries and fresh basil leaves
- Muddle them together using a muddler or the back of a spoon until the strawberries are crushed and the basil is fragrant
- Pour in the fresh lemon juice and add the honey or agave syrup to the muddled strawberries and basil
- Stir well to ensure the sweetener is fully dissolved and the flavors are well combined
- Add ice cubes to the shaker.
- Securely close the shaker and shake vigorously for about 15-20 seconds to combine all ingredients and chill the mixture thoroughly
- Fill four tall glasses with ice cubes.
- Strain the mixture equally into the prepared glasses
- Top each glass with sparkling water to add enthusiasm and volume to the mocktail
- Garnish each glass with a lemon slice, a strawberry slice, and a sprig of fresh basil for a beautiful presentation

INGREDIENTS

- 1 cup fresh strawberries, hulled and sliced
- 1/2 cup fresh lemon juice (about 3-4 lemons)
- 1/4 cup honey or agave syrup (for a vegan option)
- 1/2 cup fresh basil leaves, plus extra for garnish
- 1 cup sparkling water
- 1 cup chilled water
- Ice cubes
- Lemon slices (for garnish)
- Strawberry slices (for garnish)
- Basil sprigs (for garnish)

29

ELDERFLOWER SPRITZ

TOTAL TIME	CALORIES	SERVES
15 MINS	60 KCAL	4

DIRECTIONS

- In a large pitcher, combine the fresh lemon juice, elderflower syrup, honey or agave syrup, and chilled water
- Stir well to ensure the sweetener is fully dissolved and the flavors are well combined
- Add ice cubes to the pitcher to chill the mixture thoroughly
- Fill four tall glasses with ice cubes.
- Divide the elderflower mixture equally into the prepared glasses
- Top each glass with sparkling water to add enthusiasm and volume to the mocktail
- For a beautiful presentation, garnish each glass with a lemon slice, a sprig of fresh mint, and edible flowers

INGREDIENTS

- 1/2 cup fresh lemon juice (about 3-4 lemons)
- 1/4 cup elderflower syrup
- 1 cup sparkling water
- 1 cup chilled water
- 1/4 cup honey or agave syrup (for a vegan option)
- Ice cubes
- Lemon slices (for garnish)
- Fresh mint leaves (for garnish)
- Edible flowers (for garnish, optional)

NOTES

Freeze small mint leaves or edible flower petals in ice cubes to add a decorative and flavorful touch to your mocktail.

SUMMER
DELIGHTS

TROPICAL PARADISE

TOTAL TIME	CALORIES	SERVES
15 MINS	70 KCAL	4

INGREDIENTS

- 1 cup fresh pineapple juice (about 1 medium pineapple)
- 1/2 cup coconut water
- 1/4 cup fresh lime juice (about 2-3 limes)
- 1/4 cup mango puree (about 1 ripe mango)
- 1/4 cup honey or agave syrup (for a vegan option)
- 1/2 teaspoon grated fresh ginger
- 1 cup sparkling water
- Ice cubes
- Pineapple slices (for garnish)
- Lime slices (for garnish)
- Mint leaves (for garnish)
- Edible flowers (for garnish, optional)

DIRECTIONS

- In a blender, add the peeled and chopped mango. Blend until smooth. Strain the mango puree through a fine mesh strainer into a bowl or pitcher to remove any pulp
- In a large pitcher, combine the fresh pineapple juice, coconut water, lime juice, mango puree, honey or agave syrup, and grated fresh ginger
- Stir well to ensure the sweetener is fully dissolved and the flavors are well combined
- Add ice cubes to a cocktail shaker, pour in the mixture from the pitcher, and shake vigorously for about 15-20 seconds to combine all ingredients and chill the mixture thoroughly
- Fill four tall glasses with ice cubes
- Strain the mixture equally into the prepared glasses
- Top each glass with sparkling water to add enthusiasm and volume to the mocktail
- Garnish each glass with a pineapple slice, a lime slice, and a sprig of fresh mint for a beautiful presentation
- Add edible flowers for an extra touch of elegance

WATERMELON WAVE

INGREDIENTS

- 4 cups watermelon, cubed (seedless)

- 1/4 cup fresh lime juice (about 2-3 limes)

- 1/4 cup honey or agave syrup (for a vegan option)

- 1/2 cup coconut water

- 1 cup sparkling water

- Ice cubes

- Watermelon slices (for garnish)

- Lime slices (for garnish)

- Fresh mint leaves (for garnish)

TOTAL TIME	CALORIES	SERVES
15 MINS	50 KCAL	4

DIRECTIONS

- Add the watermelon cubes to a blender and blend until smooth. Strain the watermelon puree through a fine mesh strainer into a bowl or pitcher to remove any pulp
- n a large pitcher, combine the fresh lime juice, honey or agave syrup, coconut water, and strained watermelon puree
- Stir well to ensure the sweetener is fully dissolved and the flavors are well combined
- Add ice cubes to a cocktail shaker, pour in the mixture from the pitcher, and shake vigorously for about 15-20 seconds to combine all ingredients and chill the mixture thoroughly
- Fill four tall glasses with ice cubes.
- Strain the mixture equally into the prepared glasses
- Top each glass with sparkling water to add effervescence and volume to the mocktail
- For a beautiful presentation, garnish each glass with a slice of watermelon, a slice of lime, and a sprig of fresh mint

33

COCONUT LIME REFRESHER

TOTAL TIME	CALORIES	SERVES
15 MINS	50 KCAL	4

INGREDIENTS

- 2 cups coconut water

- 1/2 cup fresh lime juice (about 4-5 limes)

- 1/4 cup honey or agave syrup (for a vegan option)

- 1/2 cup fresh mint leaves, plus extra for garnish

- 1 cup sparkling water

- Ice cubes

- Lime slices (for garnish)

- Mint sprigs (for garnish)

DIRECTIONS

- In a large mixing glass or cocktail shaker, add the fresh mint leaves
- Muddle the mint leaves using a muddler or the back of a spoon until the mint is fragrant and slightly bruised
- Muddle the mint leaves and add the coconut water, fresh lime juice, and honey or agave syrup
- Stir well to ensure the sweetener is fully dissolved and the flavors are well combined
- Add ice cubes to the shaker
- Securely close the shaker and shake vigorously for about 15-20 seconds to combine all ingredients and chill the mixture thoroughly
- Fill four tall glasses with ice cubes.
- Strain the mixture equally into the prepared glasses
- Top each glass with sparkling water to add enthusiasm and volume to the mocktail
- Garnish each glass with a lime slice and a sprig of fresh mint for a beautiful presentation

BERRY BURST

TOTAL TIME	CALORIES	SERVES
15 MINS	60 KCAL	4

INGREDIENTS

- 1 cup fresh strawberries, hulled and sliced
- 1 cup fresh blueberries
- 1 cup fresh raspberries
- 1/4 cup fresh lemon juice (about 2 lemons)
- 1/4 cup honey or agave syrup (for a vegan option)
- 1/2 cup fresh mint leaves, plus extra for garnish
- 1 cup sparkling water
- Ice cubes
- Lemon slices (for garnish)
- Berry skewer (for garnish)

DIRECTIONS

- Add the strawberries, blueberries, raspberries, and fresh mint leaves to a large mixing glass or cocktail shaker
- Muddle them together using a muddler or the back of a spoon until the berries are crushed and the mint is fragrant
- Pour in the fresh lemon juice and add the honey or agave syrup to the muddled berries and mint
- Stir well to ensure the sweetener is fully dissolved and the flavors are well combined
- Add ice cubes to the shaker
- Securely close the shaker and shake vigorously for about 15-20 seconds to combine all ingredients and chill the mixture thoroughly
- Fill four tall glasses with ice cubes.
- Strain the mixture equally into the prepared glasses
- Top each glass with sparkling water to add enthusiasm and volume to the mocktail
- Garnish each glass with a lemon slice and a sprig of fresh mint for a beautiful presentation
- Thread a cocktail skewer with a mix of strawberries, blueberries, and raspberries for an attractive garnish

PASSION FRUIT PUNCH

TOTAL TIME	CALORIES	SERVES
15 MINS	70 KCAL	4

INGREDIENTS

- 1 cup passion fruit juice (about 4-5 passion fruits)
- 1/2 cup orange juice (about 2-3 oranges)
- 1/4 cup fresh lime juice (about 2-3 limes)
- 1/4 cup honey or agave syrup (for a vegan option)
- 1/2 cup fresh mint leaves, plus extra for garnish
- 1 cup sparkling water
- Ice cubes
- Passion fruit seeds (for garnish, optional)
- Orange slices (for garnish)
- Lime slices (for garnish)
- Mint sprigs (for garnish)

DIRECTIONS

- Cut the passion fruits in half and scoop out the pulp into a blender. Blend until smooth, then strain through a fine mesh strainer to remove the seeds, extracting the juice
- In a large mixing glass or cocktail shaker, add the fresh mint leaves
- Muddle the mint leaves using a muddler or the back of a spoon until the mint is fragrant and slightly bruised
- In a large pitcher, combine the passion fruit juice, orange juice, lime juice, and honey or agave syrup with the muddled mint
- Stir well to ensure the sweetener is fully dissolved and the flavors are well combined
- Add ice cubes to a cocktail shaker, pour in the mixture from the pitcher, and shake vigorously for about 15-20 seconds to combine all ingredients and chill the mixture thoroughly
- Fill four tall glasses with ice cubes
- Strain the mixture equally into the prepared glasses
- Top each glass with sparkling water to add enthusiasm and volume to the mocktail
- For a beautiful presentation, garnish each glass with a few passion fruit seeds, an orange slice, a lime slice, and a sprig of fresh mint

PINEAPPLE COCONUT COOLER

TOTAL TIME	CALORIES	SERVES
15 MINS	80 KCAL	4

INGREDIENTS

- 2 cups fresh pineapple juice (about 1 medium pineapple)
- 1 cup coconut milk
- 1/4 cup fresh lime juice (about 2-3 limes)
- 1/4 cup honey or agave syrup (for a vegan option)
- 1/2 cup fresh mint leaves, plus extra for garnish
- 1 cup sparkling water
- Ice cubes
- Pineapple slices (for garnish)
- Lime slices (for garnish)
- Mint sprigs (for garnish)

DIRECTIONS

- In a large mixing glass or cocktail shaker, add the fresh mint leaves
- Muddle the mint leaves using a muddler or the back of a spoon until the mint is fragrant and slightly bruised
- In a large pitcher, combine the fresh pineapple juice, coconut milk, fresh lime juice, and honey or agave syrup with the muddled mint
- Stir well to ensure the sweetener is fully dissolved and the flavors are well combined
- Add ice cubes to a cocktail shaker, pour in the mixture from the pitcher, and shake vigorously for about 15-20 seconds to combine all ingredients and chill the mixture thoroughly
- Fill four tall glasses with ice cubes
- Strain the mixture equally into the prepared glasses
- Top each glass with sparkling water to add enthusiasm and volume to the mocktail
- For a beautiful presentation, garnish each glass with a pineapple slice, a lime slice, and a sprig of fresh mint

MANGO MOJITO

TOTAL TIME	CALORIES	SERVES
15 MINS	70 KCAL	4

INGREDIENTS

- 2 ripe mangoes, peeled and cubed

- 1/2 cup fresh lime juice (about 4-5 limes)

- 1/4 cup honey or agave syrup (for a vegan option)

- 1/2 cup fresh mint leaves, plus extra for garnish

- 1 cup sparkling water

- Ice cubes

- Mango slices (for garnish)

- Lime slices (for garnish)

- Mint sprigs (for garnish)

DIRECTIONS

- Blend the cubed mangoes in a blender until smooth, then strain the mango puree through a fine mesh strainer into a bowl or pitcher to remove any pulp

- In a large mixing glass or cocktail shaker, add the fresh mint leaves

- Muddle the mint leaves using a muddler or the back of a spoon until the mint is fragrant and slightly bruised

- Add the mango puree, fresh lime juice, and honey or agave syrup to the muddled mint leaves

- Stir well to ensure the sweetener is fully dissolved and the flavors are well combined

- Add ice cubes to the shaker.

- Securely close the shaker and shake vigorously for about 15-20 seconds to combine all ingredients and chill the mixture thoroughly

- Fill four tall glasses with ice cubes.

- Strain the mixture equally into the prepared glasses

- Top each glass with sparkling water to add enthusiasm and volume to the mocktail

- Garnish each glass with a mango slice, a lime slice, and a sprig of fresh mint for a beautiful presentation

CITRUS SPLASH

TOTAL TIME	CALORIES	SERVES
15 MINS	**60 KCAL**	**4**

INGREDIENTS

- 1 cup fresh orange juice (about 2-3 oranges)
- 1/2 cup fresh lemon juice (about 4-5 lemons)
- 1/2 cup fresh lime juice (about 4-5 limes)
- 1/4 cup honey or agave syrup (for a vegan option)
- 1/2 cup fresh mint leaves, plus extra for garnish
- 1 cup sparkling water
- Ice cubes
- Orange slices (for garnish)
- Lemon slices (for garnish)
- Lime slices (for garnish)

DIRECTIONS

- In a large mixing glass or cocktail shaker, add the fresh mint leaves
- Muddle the mint leaves using a muddler or the back of a spoon until the mint is fragrant and slightly bruised
- In a large pitcher, mix together the fresh orange juice, lemon juice, lime juice, honey or agave syrup, and crushed mint
- Stir well to ensure the sweetener is fully dissolved and the flavors are well combined
- Add ice cubes to a cocktail shaker, pour in the mixture from the pitcher, and shake vigorously for about 15-20 seconds to combine all ingredients and chill the mixture thoroughly
- Fill four tall glasses with ice cubes
- Strain the mixture equally into the prepared glasses
- Top each glass with sparkling water to add effervescence and volume to the mocktail
- For a beautiful presentation, garnish each glass with an orange slice, a lemon slice, a lime slice, and a sprig of fresh mint

RASPBERRY LEMONADE

TOTAL TIME	CALORIES	SERVES
15 MINS	50 KCAL	4

INGREDIENTS

- 1 cup fresh raspberries
- 1/2 cup fresh lemon juice (about 4-5 lemons)
- 1/4 cup honey or agave syrup (for a vegan option)
- 2 cups chilled water
- 1 cup sparkling water
- Ice cubes
- Lemon slices (for garnish)
- Fresh mint leaves (for garnish)

DIRECTIONS

- In a large mixing glass or cocktail shaker, add the fresh raspberries
- Muddle the raspberries using a muddler or the back of a spoon until they are crushed and release their juices
- Combine the fresh lemon juice, honey or agave syrup, and muddled raspberries in a large pitcher
- Stir well to ensure the sweetener is fully dissolved and the flavors are well combined
- Add the chilled water to the pitcher and stir to combine
- Add ice cubes to the shaker, pour in the mixture from the pitcher, and shake vigorously for about 15-20 seconds to combine all ingredients and chill the mixture thoroughly
- Fill four tall glasses with ice cubes
- Strain the mixture equally into the prepared glasses
- Top each glass with sparkling water to add enthusiasm and volume to the mocktail
- Garnish each glass with a lemon slice and a sprig of fresh mint for a beautiful presentation

PEACHY KEEN

TOTAL TIME	CALORIES	SERVES
15 MINS	60 KCAL	4

DIRECTIONS

- Add the peeled and sliced peaches to a blender. Blend until smooth. Strain the peach puree through a fine mesh strainer into a bowl or pitcher to remove any pulp
- In a large mixing glass or cocktail shaker, add the fresh mint leaves
- Muddle the mint leaves using a muddler or the back of a spoon until the mint is fragrant and slightly bruised
- Muddle the mint leaves and add the peach puree, fresh lemon juice, and honey or agave syrup
- Stir well to ensure the sweetener is fully dissolved and the flavors are well combined
- Add ice cubes to the shaker
- Securely close the shaker and shake vigorously for about 15-20 seconds to combine all ingredients and chill the mixture thoroughly
- Fill four tall glasses with ice cubes.
- Strain the mixture equally into the prepared glasses
- Top each glass with sparkling water to add enthusiasm and volume to the mocktail
- For a beautiful presentation, garnish each glass with a peach slice, a lemon slice, and a sprig of fresh mint

INGREDIENTS

- 2 ripe peaches, peeled and sliced
- 1/2 cup fresh lemon juice (about 3-4 lemons)
- 1/4 cup honey or agave syrup (for a vegan option)
- 1/2 cup fresh mint leaves, plus extra for garnish
- 1 cup sparkling water
- 1 cup chilled water
- Ice cubes
- Peach slices (for garnish)
- Lemon slices (for garnish)
- Mint sprigs (for garnish)

FROZEN BANANA SMOOTHIE

TOTAL TIME	CALORIES	SERVES
15 MINS	120 KCAL	4

DIRECTIONS

- Peel and freeze the bananas ahead of time. This will give the smoothie a creamy texture
- In a blender, add the frozen bananas, coconut milk, fresh orange juice, honey or agave syrup, vanilla extract, and Greek yogurt if using
- Blend until smooth and creamy. If a thicker texture is desired, add a few ice cubes and blend again
- Taste the smoothie and adjust the sweetness by adding more honey or agave syrup if needed. Blend again to mix
- Pour the smoothie into four tall glasses
- Garnish each glass with a fresh banana slice and a sprig of mint for a beautiful presentation

INGREDIENTS

- 3 ripe bananas, peeled and frozen
- 1 cup coconut milk (or any preferred milk alternative)
- 1/2 cup fresh orange juice
- 1/4 cup honey or agave syrup (for a vegan option)
- 1/2 teaspoon vanilla extract
- 1/2 cup Greek yogurt (optional for creaminess)
- Ice cubes (optional for extra thickness)
- Fresh banana slices (for garnish)
- Mint leaves (for garnish)

NOTES

- Protein: 3g
- Vitamin C: 20% DV
- Calcium: 4% DV

LIME CUCUMBER COOLER

TOTAL TIME	CALORIES	SERVES
15 MINS	50 KCAL	4

INGREDIENTS

- 2 cucumbers, peeled and sliced
- 1/2 cup fresh lime juice (about 4-5 limes)
- 1/4 cup honey or agave syrup (for a vegan option)
- 1 cup coconut water
- 1/2 cup fresh mint leaves, plus extra for garnish
- 2 cups ice cubes
- Lime slices (for garnish)
- Cucumber slices (for garnish)
- Mint sprigs (for garnish)

DIRECTIONS

- Peel and slice the cucumbers.
- Juice the limes to get 1/2 cup of fresh lime juice
- In a blender, add the cucumber slices, fresh lime juice, honey or agave syrup, coconut water, fresh mint leaves, and ice cubes
- Blend until smooth and well combined
- Taste the mixture and adjust the sweetness by adding more honey or agave syrup if needed. Blend again to mix
- Pour the mixture into four tall glasses
- For a beautiful presentation, garnish each glass with a lime slice, a cucumber slice, and a sprig of fresh mint

NOTES

Replace honey or agave syrup with a sugar-free sweetener such as stevia or monk fruit sweetener

BLUE LAGOON

TOTAL TIME	CALORIES	SERVES
10 MINS	70 KCAL	4

INGREDIENTS

- 2 cups fresh pineapple juice
- 1 cup fresh lemon juice (about 6-8 lemons)
- 1/4 cup blue curaçao syrup (non-alcoholic)
- 1/4 cup honey or agave syrup (for a vegan option)
- 1 cup coconut water
- 1/2 cup fresh mint leaves, plus extra for garnish
- Ice cubes
- Lemon slices (for garnish)
- Pineapple chunks (for garnish)
- Mint sprigs (for garnish)

DIRECTIONS

- In a large mixing glass or cocktail shaker, add the fresh mint leaves
- Muddle the mint leaves using a muddler or the back of a spoon until the mint is fragrant and slightly bruised
- In a large pitcher, combine the fresh pineapple juice, lemon juice, blue curaçao syrup, honey or agave syrup, and coconut water with the muddled mint
- Stir well to ensure the sweetener is fully dissolved and the flavors are well combined
- Add ice cubes to the shaker
- Securely close the shaker and shake vigorously for about 15-20 seconds to combine all ingredients and chill the mixture thoroughly
- Fill four tall glasses with ice cubes
- Strain the mixture equally into the prepared glasses
- For a beautiful presentation, garnish each glass with a lemon slice, a pineapple chunk, and a sprig of fresh mint

KIWI PUNCH

TOTAL TIME	CALORIES	SERVES
15 MINS	**70 KCAL**	**4**

DIRECTIONS

- In a blender, add the peeled and chopped kiwis. Blend until smooth. Strain the kiwi puree through a fine mesh strainer into a bowl or pitcher to remove any pulp
- In a large mixing glass or cocktail shaker, add the fresh mint leaves
- Muddle the mint leaves using a muddler or the back of a spoon until the mint is fragrant and slightly bruised
- Muddle the mint leaves and add the kiwi puree, fresh lime juice, honey or agave syrup, and pineapple juice
- Stir well to ensure the sweetener is fully dissolved and the flavors are well combined
- Add ice cubes to the shaker
- Securely close the shaker and shake vigorously for about 15-20 seconds to combine all ingredients and chill the mixture thoroughly
- Fill four tall glasses with ice cubes.
- Strain the mixture equally into the prepared glasses
- Top each glass with sparkling water to add effervescence and volume to the mocktail
- Garnish each glass with a kiwi slice, a lime slice, and a sprig of fresh mint for a beautiful presentation

INGREDIENTS

- 6 ripe kiwis, peeled and chopped
- 1/2 cup fresh lime juice (about 4-5 limes)
- 1/4 cup honey or agave syrup (for a vegan option)
- 1 cup pineapple juice
- 1 cup sparkling water
- 1/2 cup fresh mint leaves, plus extra for garnish
- Ice cubes
- Kiwi slices (for garnish)
- Lime slices (for garnish)
- Mint sprigs (for garnish)

CHERRY LIMEADE

INGREDIENTS

- 2 cups fresh cherries, pitted and halved (or 1 cup cherry juice)

- 1/2 cup fresh lime juice (about 4-5 limes)

- 1/4 cup honey or agave syrup (for a vegan option)

- 1 cup sparkling water

- 1/2 cup fresh mint leaves, plus extra for garnish

- Ice cubes

- Lime slices (for garnish)

- Fresh cherries (for garnish)

TOTAL TIME	CALORIES	SERVES
15 MINS	70 KCAL	4

DIRECTIONS

- In a large mixing glass or cocktail shaker, add the fresh cherries and mint leaves
- Muddle them together using a muddler or the back of a spoon until the cherries are crushed and the mint is fragrant
- Add the fresh lime juice and honey or agave syrup to the muddled cherries and mint
- Stir well to ensure the sweetener is fully dissolved and the flavors are well combined
- Add ice cubes to the shaker
- Securely close the shaker and shake vigorously for about 15-20 seconds to combine all ingredients and chill the mixture thoroughly
- Fill four tall glasses with ice cubes.
- Strain the mixture equally into the prepared glasses
- Top each glass with sparkling water to add enthusiasm and volume to the mocktail
- Garnish each glass with a lime slice and a fresh cherry for a beautiful presentation

STRAWBERRY WATERMELON SLUSHIE

TOTAL TIME	CALORIES	SERVES
10 MINS	70 KCAL	4

DIRECTIONS

- Cube and freeze the watermelon and strawberries ahead of time. This will give the slushie a frosty texture
- In a blender, add the frozen watermelon, frozen strawberries, fresh lime juice, honey or agave syrup, and coconut water
- Blend until smooth and slushy. If a thicker texture is desired, add a few ice cubes and blend again
- Taste the slushie and adjust the sweetness by adding more honey or agave syrup if needed. Blend again to mix
- Pour the slushie mixture into four tall glasses
- For a beautiful presentation, garnish each glass with a slice of watermelon, a slice of strawberry, and a sprig of fresh mint

INGREDIENTS

- 3 cups fresh watermelon, cubed and frozen
- 1 cup fresh strawberries, hulled and frozen
- 1/4 cup fresh lime juice (about 2-3 limes)
- 1/4 cup honey or agave syrup (for a vegan option)
- 1 cup coconut water
- Ice cubes (optional, for extra thickness)
- Fresh mint leaves (for garnish)
- Watermelon slices (for garnish)
- Strawberry slices (for garnish)

NOTES

- Vitamin C: 50% DV
- Calcium: 2% DV
- Iron: 2% DV

PINEAPPLE MINT FIZZ

TOTAL TIME	CALORIES	SERVES
10 MINS	70 KCAL	4

INGREDIENTS

- 2 cups fresh pineapple juice
- 1/2 cup fresh lime juice (about 4-5 limes)
- 1/4 cup honey or agave syrup (for a vegan option)
- 1 cup sparkling water
- 1/2 cup fresh mint leaves, plus extra for garnish
- Ice cubes
- Pineapple slices (for garnish)
- Lime slices (for garnish)
- Mint sprigs (for garnish)

DIRECTIONS

- In a large mixing glass or cocktail shaker, add the fresh mint leaves
- Muddle the mint leaves using a muddler or the back of a spoon until the mint is fragrant and slightly bruised
- Add the fresh pineapple juice, lime juice, and honey or agave syrup to the muddled mint leaves
- Stir well to ensure the sweetener is fully dissolved and the flavors are well combined
- Add ice cubes to the shaker
- Securely close the shaker and shake vigorously for about 15-20 seconds to combine all ingredients and chill the mixture thoroughly
- Fill four tall glasses with ice cubes
- Strain the mixture equally into the prepared glasses
- Top each glass with sparkling water to add enthusiasm and volume to the mocktail
- Garnish each glass with a pineapple slice, a lime slice, and a sprig of fresh mint for a beautiful presentation

PINA COLADA MOCKTAIL

TOTAL TIME	CALORIES	SERVES
10 MINS	120 KCAL	4

DIRECTIONS

- Ensure all ingredients are chilled for the best refreshing effect
- Optional: Freeze the pineapple chunks ahead of time for an extra frosty mocktail
- In a blender, add the fresh pineapple juice, coconut milk, honey or agave syrup, crushed ice, fresh pineapple chunks (if using), and vanilla extract
- Blend until smooth and creamy
- Taste the mixture and adjust the sweetness by adding more honey or agave syrup if needed. Blend again to mix
- Pour the Pina Colada mocktail into four tall glasses
- For a beautiful presentation, garnish each glass with a pineapple slice, a maraschino cherry, and a sprig of fresh mint

INGREDIENTS

- 2 cups fresh pineapple juice

- 1 cup coconut milk

- 1/4 cup honey or agave syrup

  (for a vegan option)

- 1/2 cup crushed ice

- 1/2 cup fresh pineapple chunks

  (optional, for texture)

- 1/2 teaspoon vanilla extract

- Pineapple slices (for garnish)

- Maraschino cherries (for garnish)

- Fresh mint leaves (for garnish)

NOTES

- Vitamin C: 60% DV
- Calcium: 2% DV
- Iron: 2% DV

SUMMER SUNSET

TOTAL TIME	CALORIES	SERVES
15 MINS	80 KCAL	4

INGREDIENTS

- 1 cup fresh orange juice (about 2-3 oranges)
- 1 cup fresh pineapple juice
- 1/2 cup fresh strawberry puree (about 1 cup strawberries, blended and strained)
- 1/4 cup fresh lime juice (about 2-3 limes)
- 1/4 cup honey or agave syrup (for a vegan option)
- 1 cup sparkling water
- Ice cubes
- Orange slices (for garnish)
- Pineapple chunks (for garnish)
- Fresh mint leaves (for garnish)

DIRECTIONS

- In a blender, add the fresh strawberries. Blend until smooth, then strain through a fine mesh strainer to remove seeds and pulp
- In a large pitcher, combine fresh orange juice, pineapple juice, strawberry puree, lime juice, and honey or agave syrup
- Stir well to ensure the sweetener is fully dissolved and the flavors are well combined
- Add ice cubes to a cocktail shaker, pour in the mixture from the pitcher, and shake vigorously for about 15-20 seconds to combine all ingredients and chill the mixture thoroughly
- Fill four tall glasses with ice cubes
- Strain the mixture equally into the prepared glasses
- Top each glass with sparkling water to add effervescence and volume to the mocktail
- For a beautiful presentation, garnish each glass with an orange slice, a pineapple chunk, and a sprig of fresh mint

GRAPEFRUIT COOLER

INGREDIENTS

- 2 cups fresh grapefruit juice (about 2-3 grapefruits)
- 1/2 cup fresh lime juice (about 4-5 limes)
- 1/4 cup honey or agave syrup (for a vegan option)
- 1 cup sparkling water
- 1/2 cup fresh mint leaves, plus extra for garnish
- Ice cubes
- Grapefruit slices (for garnish)
- Lime slices (for garnish)
- Mint sprigs (for garnish)

TOTAL TIME	CALORIES	SERVES
15 MINS	60 KCAL	4

DIRECTIONS

- In a large mixing glass or cocktail shaker, add the fresh mint leaves
- Muddle the mint leaves using a muddler or the back of a spoon until the mint is fragrant and slightly bruised
- Add the fresh grapefruit juice, lime juice, and honey or agave syrup to the muddled mint leaves
- Stir well to ensure the sweetener is fully dissolved and the flavors are well combined
- Add ice cubes to the shaker
- Securely close the shaker and shake vigorously for about 15-20 seconds to combine all ingredients and chill the mixture thoroughly
- Fill four tall glasses with ice cubes.
- Strain the mixture equally into the prepared glasses
- Top each glass with sparkling water to add effervescence and volume to the mocktail
- Garnish each glass with a grapefruit slice, a lime slice, and a sprig of fresh mint for a beautiful presentation

NOTES

Vitamin C: 50% DV

LEMONADE STAND

TOTAL TIME	CALORIES	SERVES
15 MINS	50 KCAL	4

INGREDIENTS

- 1 cup fresh lemon juice (about 6-8 lemons)
- 1/2 cup fresh lime juice (about 4-5 limes)
- 1/4 cup honey or agave syrup (for a vegan option)
- 2 cups cold water
- 1 cup sparkling water
- 1/2 cup fresh mint leaves, plus extra for garnish
- Ice cubes
- Lemon slices (for garnish)
- Lime slices (for garnish)
- Fresh mint sprigs (for garnish)

DIRECTIONS

- In a large mixing glass or cocktail shaker, add the fresh mint leaves
- Muddle the mint leaves using a muddler or the back of a spoon until the mint is fragrant and slightly bruised
- In a large pitcher, combine the fresh lemon juice, lime juice, and honey or agave syrup
- Stir well to ensure the sweetener is fully dissolved and the flavors are well combined
- Add the cold water to the pitcher and stir to combine
- Add ice cubes to the shaker, pour in the mixture from the pitcher, and shake vigorously for about 15-20 seconds to combine all ingredients and chill the mixture thoroughly
- Fill four tall glasses with ice cubes
- Strain the mixture equally into the prepared glasses
- Top each glass with sparkling water to add effervescence and volume to the mocktail
- For a beautiful presentation, garnish each glass with a lemon slice, a lime slice, and a sprig of fresh mint

TROPICAL BREEZE

TOTAL TIME	CALORIES	SERVES
15 MINS	80 KCAL	4

DIRECTIONS

- In a large pitcher, combine the fresh pineapple juice, orange juice, coconut water, fresh lime juice, honey or agave syrup, and grated fresh ginger
- Stir well to ensure the sweetener is fully dissolved and the flavors are well combined
- Add ice cubes to a cocktail shaker, pour in the mixture from the pitcher, and shake vigorously for about 15-20 seconds to combine all ingredients and chill the mixture thoroughly
- Fill four tall glasses with ice cubes
- Strain the mixture equally into the prepared glasses
- Top each glass with sparkling water to add effervescence and volume to the mocktail
- Finally, garnish each glass with a pineapple slice, an orange slice, and a sprig of fresh mint for a beautiful presentation. Enjoy your refreshing mocktail

INGREDIENTS

- 1 cup fresh pineapple juice
- 1 cup fresh orange juice
- 1/2 cup coconut water
- 1/4 cup fresh lime juice (about 2-3 limes)
- 1/4 cup honey or agave syrup (for a vegan option)
- 1/2 teaspoon grated fresh ginger
- 1 cup sparkling water
- Ice cubes
- Pineapple slices (for garnish)
- Orange slices (for garnish)
- Fresh mint leaves (for garnish)

NOTES

- Vitamin C: 70% DV
- Calcium: 2% DV
- Iron: 2% DV

AUTUMN
WARMERS

APPLE CIDER SPARKLER

INGREDIENTS

- 2 cups apple cider
- 1/2 cup fresh orange juice
- 1/4 cup fresh lemon juice
- 1/4 cup honey or agave syrup (for a vegan option)
- 1/2 teaspoon ground cinnamon
- 1/4 teaspoon ground nutmeg
- 1 cup sparkling water
- Ice cubes
- Apple slices (for garnish)
- Orange slices (for garnish)
- Cinnamon sticks (for garnish)

TOTAL TIME	CALORIES	SERVES
15 MINS	80 KCAL	4

DIRECTIONS

- Combine the apple cider, fresh orange juice, lemon juice, honey or agave syrup, ground cinnamon, and ground nutmeg in a large pitcher. Stir well to ensure the sweetener and spices are fully dissolved and the flavors are well combined.
- Add ice cubes to a cocktail shaker, pour in the mixture from the pitcher, and shake vigorously for about 15-20 seconds to combine all ingredients and chill the mixture thoroughly
- Fill four tall glasses with ice cubes
- Strain the mixture equally into the prepared glasses
- Top each glass with sparkling water to add enthusiasm and volume to the mocktail
- For a beautiful presentation, garnish each glass with an apple slice, an orange slice, and a cinnamon stick

NOTES

Sugar-Free Option: Replace honey or agave syrup with a sugar-free sweetener such as stevia or monk fruit sweetener

PUMPKIN SPICE DELIGHT

TOTAL TIME	CALORIES	SERVES
15 MINS	90 KCAL	4

INGREDIENTS

- 1 cup pumpkin puree
- 2 cups apple cider
- 1/2 cup fresh orange juice
- 1/4 cup honey or agave syrup (for a vegan option)
- 1 teaspoon pumpkin pie spice (a blend of cinnamon, nutmeg, ginger, and cloves)
- 1 teaspoon vanilla extract
- 1 cup sparkling water
- Ice cubes
- Cinnamon sticks (for garnish)
- Orange slices (for garnish)
- Whipped cream (optional, for garnish)
- Ground cinnamon (for garnish)

DIRECTIONS

- In a large pitcher, combine the pumpkin puree, apple cider, fresh orange juice, honey or agave syrup, pumpkin pie spice, and vanilla extract
- Stir well to ensure the sweetener and spices are fully dissolved, and the flavors are well combined
- Transfer the mixture to a blender and blend until smooth and well-mixed
- Add ice cubes to a cocktail shaker, pour in the blended mixture, and shake vigorously for about 15-20 seconds to combine all ingredients and chill the mixture thoroughly
- Fill four tall glasses with ice cubes
- Strain the mixture equally into the prepared glasses
- Top each glass with sparkling water to add enthusiasm and volume to the mocktail
- If desired, garnish each glass with a cinnamon stick, an orange slice, and a dollop of whipped cream. Sprinkle a pinch of ground cinnamon on top for an extra touch

CRANBERRY ORANGE PUNCH

TOTAL TIME	CALORIES	SERVES
15 MINS	70 KCAL	4

DIRECTIONS

- Blend fresh cranberries in a blender until smooth, then strain the puree to remove any pulp
- Combine cranberry juice, fresh orange juice, cranberry puree, honey or agave syrup, and grated fresh ginger in a large pitcher. Stir well to dissolve the sweetener and ginger
- Add ice cubes to a cocktail shaker, pour in the mixture from the pitcher, and shake vigorously for about 15-20 seconds to combine all ingredients and chill the mixture thoroughly
- Fill four tall glasses with ice cubes and strain the mixture equally into the prepared glasses
- Top each glass with sparkling water for enthusiasm and volume
- Garnish each glass with an orange slice, a few fresh cranberries, and a sprig of fresh mint for a beautiful presentation

INGREDIENTS

- 1 cup fresh cranberries
- 2 cups cranberry juice (unsweetened)
- 1 cup fresh orange juice (about 3-4 oranges)
- 1/4 cup honey or agave syrup (for a vegan option)
- 1 teaspoon grated fresh ginger
- 1 cup sparkling water
- Ice cubes
- Orange slices (for garnish)
- Fresh cranberries (for garnish)
- Fresh mint leaves (for garnish)

NOTES

Vitamin C: 40% DV

CINNAMON PEAR FIZZ

TOTAL TIME	CALORIES	SERVES
15 MINS	70 KCAL	4

INGREDIENTS

- 2 ripe pears, peeled and chopped
- 1 cup pear juice
- 1/2 cup fresh lemon juice (about 3-4 lemons)
- 1/4 cup honey or agave syrup (for a vegan option)
- 1 teaspoon ground cinnamon
- 1 cup sparkling water
- Ice cubes
- Pear slices (for garnish)
- Cinnamon sticks (for garnish)
- Fresh mint leaves (for garnish)

DIRECTIONS

- Start by placing the chopped pears in a blender and blending until smooth. Then, strain the pear puree through a fine mesh strainer into a bowl or pitcher to remove any pulp
- In a large pitcher, mix together the pear juice, fresh lemon juice, pear puree, honey or agave syrup, and ground cinnamon. Stir well to ensure that the sweetener and cinnamon are fully dissolved and the flavors are well combined
- Next, add ice cubes to a cocktail shaker, pour in the mixture from the pitcher, and shake vigorously for about 15-20 seconds to combine all the ingredients and thoroughly chill the mixture
- Fill four tall glasses with ice cubes
- Strain the mixture equally into the prepared glasses
- Top each glass with sparkling water to add enthusiasm and volume to the mocktail
- Finally, garnish each glass with a pear slice, a cinnamon stick, and a sprig of fresh mint for a beautiful presentation

MAPLE APPLE COOLER

TOTAL TIME	CALORIES	SERVES
15 MINS	80 KCAL	4

INGREDIENTS

- 2 cups fresh apple cider
- 1/2 cup fresh lemon juice (about 4-5 lemons)
- 1/4 cup pure maple syrup
- 1/2 teaspoon ground cinnamon
- 1 cup sparkling water
- Ice cubes
- Apple slices (for garnish)
- Lemon slices (for garnish)
- Fresh mint leaves (for garnish)

DIRECTIONS

- Combine the fresh apple cider, lemon juice, pure maple syrup, and ground cinnamon in a large pitcher
- Stir well to ensure the maple syrup and cinnamon are fully dissolved and the flavors are well combined
- Add ice cubes to a cocktail shaker, pour in the mixture from the pitcher, and shake vigorously for about 15-20 seconds to combine all ingredients and chill the mixture thoroughly
- Fill four tall glasses with ice cubes
- Strain the mixture equally into the prepared glasses
- Top each glass with sparkling water to add enthusiasm and volume to the mocktail
- For a beautiful presentation, garnish each glass with an apple slice, a lemon slice, and a sprig of fresh mint

NOTES

Sugar-Free Option:
Replace maple syrup with a sugar-free sweetener such as stevia or monk fruit sweetener

GINGER SNAP

TOTAL TIME	CALORIES	SERVES
15 MINS	70 KCAL	4

INGREDIENTS

- 1 cup fresh ginger root, peeled and sliced
- 2 cups apple cider
- 1/2 cup fresh lemon juice (about 4-5 lemons)
- 1/4 cup honey or agave syrup (for a vegan option)
- 1 teaspoon ground cinnamon
- 1/4 teaspoon ground cloves
- 1 cup sparkling water
- Ice cubes
- Lemon slices (for garnish)
- Apple slices (for garnish)
- Fresh mint leaves (for garnish)

DIRECTIONS

- In a small saucepan, add the sliced ginger and 1 cup of water
- Bring to a boil, then reduce the heat and let it simmer for 10 minutes
- Strain the ginger slices out, reserving the liquid
- In a large pitcher, combine the apple cider, fresh lemon juice, honey or agave syrup, ground cinnamon, ground cloves, and ginger syrup
- Stir well to ensure the sweetener and spices are fully dissolved, and the flavors are well combined
- Add ice cubes to a cocktail shaker, pour in the mixture from the pitcher, and shake vigorously for about 15-20 seconds to combine all ingredients and chill the mixture thoroughly
- Fill four tall glasses with ice cubes
- Strain the mixture equally into the prepared glasses
- Top each glass with sparkling water to add enthusiasm and volume to the mocktail
- Garnish each glass with a lemon slice, an apple slice, and a sprig of fresh mint for a beautiful presentation

CARAMEL APPLE MOCKTAIL

TOTAL TIME	CALORIES	SERVES
15 MINS	90 KCAL	4

INGREDIENTS

- 2 cups apple cider
- 1/2 cup fresh lemon juice (about 4-5 lemons)
- 1/4 cup caramel syrup (store-bought or homemade)
- 1 teaspoon ground cinnamon
- 1 teaspoon vanilla extract
- 1 cup sparkling water
- Ice cubes
- Apple slices (for garnish)
- Cinnamon sticks (for garnish)
- Caramel drizzle (for garnish)
- Whipped cream (optional, for garnish)

DIRECTIONS

- Combine the apple cider, fresh lemon juice, caramel syrup, ground cinnamon, and vanilla extract in a large pitcher
- Stir well to ensure the caramel syrup and cinnamon are fully dissolved, and the flavors are well combined
- Add ice cubes to a cocktail shaker, pour in the mixture from the pitcher, and shake vigorously for about 15-20 seconds to combine all ingredients and chill the mixture thoroughly
- Fill four tall glasses with ice cubes
- Strain the mixture equally into the prepared glasses
- Top each glass with sparkling water to add effervescence and volume to the mocktail
- Garnish each glass with an apple slice and a cinnamon stick
- Drizzle caramel syrup around the rim of the glass and, if desired, add a dollop of whipped cream on top

NOTES

Dairy-Free Option: Use a dairy-free caramel syrup and whipped cream if opting for the whipped cream garnish

FIG AND HONEY FIZZ

INGREDIENTS

- 4 fresh figs, quartered
- 2 cups sparkling water
- 1/2 cup fresh lemon juice (about 4-5 lemons)
- 1/4 cup honey or agave syrup (for a vegan option)
- 1 teaspoon vanilla extract
- 1/2 teaspoon ground cinnamon
- Ice cubes
- Lemon slices (for garnish)
- Fresh fig slices (for garnish)
- Fresh thyme sprigs (for garnish)

TOTAL TIME	CALORIES	SERVES
15 MINS	70 KCAL	4

DIRECTIONS

- In a large mixing glass or cocktail shaker, add the quartered fresh figs.
- Muddle the figs using a muddler or the back of a spoon until they are thoroughly crushed and release their juices
- Add the fresh lemon juice, honey or agave syrup, vanilla extract, and ground cinnamon to the muddled figs
- Stir well to ensure the honey and cinnamon are fully dissolved and the flavors are well combined
- Add ice cubes to the shaker, pour in the mixture from the mixing glass, and shake vigorously for about 15-20 seconds to combine all ingredients and chill the mixture thoroughly
- Fill four tall glasses with ice cubes
- Strain the mixture equally into the prepared glasses, ensuring to leave the fig pulp behind
- Top each glass with sparkling water to add enthusiasm and volume to the mocktail
- Garnish each glass with a lemon slice, a fresh fig slice, and a sprig of fresh thyme for a beautiful presentation

SPICED POMEGRANATE PUNCH

TOTAL TIME	CALORIES	SERVES
15 MINS	70 KCAL	4

DIRECTIONS

- Combine the pomegranate juice, fresh orange juice, lemon juice, and honey or agave syrup in a large pitcher
- Stir well to ensure the sweetener is fully dissolved
- Add the ground cinnamon, ground cloves, and ground nutmeg to the juice mixture
- Stir thoroughly to ensure the spices are evenly distributed
- Add ice cubes to a cocktail shaker, pour in the spiced juice mixture from the pitcher, and shake vigorously for about 15-20 seconds to combine all ingredients and chill the mixture thoroughly
- Fill four tall glasses with ice cubes
- Strain the mixture equally into the prepared glasses
- Top each glass with sparkling water to add effervescence and volume to the mocktail
- For a beautiful presentation, garnish each glass with a few pomegranate seeds, an orange slice, and a cinnamon stick

NOTES
- Vitamin C: 35% DV

INGREDIENTS

- 2 cups pomegranate juice
- 1 cup fresh orange juice (about 3-4 oranges)
- 1/2 cup fresh lemon juice (about 4-5 lemons)
- 1/4 cup honey or agave syrup (for a vegan option)
- 1 teaspoon ground cinnamon
- 1/2 teaspoon ground cloves
- 1/2 teaspoon ground nutmeg
- 1 cup sparkling water
- Ice cubes
- Pomegranate seeds (for garnish)
- Orange slices (for garnish)
- Cinnamon sticks (for garnish)

PEAR GINGER REFRESHER

TOTAL TIME	CALORIES	SERVES
15 MINS	80 KCAL	4

INGREDIENTS

- 2 ripe pears, peeled and chopped
- 1 cup pear juice
- 1/2 cup fresh lemon juice (about 4-5 lemons)
- 1/4 cup honey or agave syrup (for a vegan option)
- 1 tablespoon freshly grated ginger
- 1 cup sparkling water
- Ice cubes
- Pear slices (for garnish)
- Lemon slices (for garnish)
- Fresh mint leaves (for garnish)

DIRECTIONS

- In a blender, add the chopped pears and blend until smooth. Strain the pear puree through a fine mesh strainer into a bowl or pitcher to remove any pulp
- In a large pitcher, combine the pear juice, fresh lemon juice, pear puree, honey or agave syrup, and freshly grated ginger
- Stir well to ensure the honey and ginger are fully dissolved and the flavors are well combined
- Add ice cubes to a cocktail shaker, pour in the mixture from the pitcher, and shake vigorously for about 15-20 seconds to combine all ingredients and chill the mixture thoroughly
- Fill four tall glasses with ice cubes
- Strain the mixture equally into the prepared glasses
- Top each glass with sparkling water to add enthusiasm and volume to the mocktail
- For a beautiful presentation, garnish each glass with a pear slice, a lemon slice, and a sprig of fresh mint

NOTES

Replace honey or agave syrup with a sugar-free sweetener such as stevia or monk fruit sweetener

PUMPKIN PIE SMOOTHIE

TOTAL TIME	CALORIES	SERVES
10 MINS	120 KCAL	4

DIRECTIONS

- Blend the pumpkin puree, almond milk, Greek yogurt, honey or maple syrup, pumpkin pie spice, vanilla extract, and frozen banana
- Blend the ingredients on high speed until smooth and creamy. For a thicker texture, add a few ice cubes and blend again
- Taste the smoothie and adjust the sweetness by adding more honey or maple syrup if needed. Blend again to mix
- Divide the Pumpkin Pie Smoothie into four glasses
- Add a dollop of whipped cream on the top of each glass if desired
- Sprinkle ground cinnamon on top for added flavor
- Finish by topping each glass with a sprinkle of crushed graham crackers for a pie-like touch

INGREDIENTS

- 1 cup pumpkin puree
- 2 cups almond milk (or any preferred milk alternative)
- 1/2 cup Greek yogurt (for creaminess)
- 1/4 cup honey or maple syrup (for a vegan option)
- 1 teaspoon pumpkin pie spice
- 1 teaspoon vanilla extract
- 1 frozen banana (for added creaminess)
- Ice cubes (optional, for extra thickness)
- Whipped cream (optional, for garnish)
- Ground cinnamon (for garnish)
- Crushed graham crackers (for garnish)

NOTES

- Dairy-Free Option: Use a dairy-free yogurt alternative and ensure the whipped cream, if used, is also dairy-free

AUTUMN HARVEST

TOTAL TIME	CALORIES	SERVES
15 MINS	80 KCAL	4

DIRECTIONS

- In a large pitcher, combine the apple cider, pear juice, cranberry juice, and fresh lemon juice
- Add the honey or agave syrup and stir well to ensure the sweetener is fully dissolved
- Add the ground cinnamon, ground nutmeg, and ground cloves to the juice mixture
- Stir thoroughly to ensure the spices are evenly distributed
- Add ice cubes to a cocktail shaker, pour in the spiced juice mixture from the pitcher, and shake vigorously for about 15-20 seconds to combine all ingredients and chill the mixture thoroughly
- Fill four tall glasses with ice cubes
- Strain the mixture equally into the prepared glasses
- Top each glass with sparkling water to add enthusiasm and volume to the mocktail
- For a beautiful presentation, garnish each glass with apple slices, pear slices, fresh cranberries, and a sprig of fresh mint

INGREDIENTS

- 1 cup apple cider
- 1 cup pear juice
- 1/2 cup cranberry juice (unsweetened)
- 1/4 cup fresh lemon juice (about 2-3 lemons)
- 1/4 cup honey or agave syrup (for a vegan option)
- 1 teaspoon ground cinnamon
- 1/2 teaspoon ground nutmeg
- 1/4 teaspoon ground cloves
- 1 cup sparkling water
- Ice cubes
- Apple slices (for garnish)
- Pear slices (for garnish)
- Fresh cranberries (for garnish)
- Fresh mint leaves (for garnish)

NOTES

Vitamin C: 25% DV

CHAI LATTE MOCKTAIL

TOTAL TIME	CALORIES	SERVES
15 MINS	80 KCAL	4

INGREDIENTS

- 2 cups brewed chai tea (strong, chilled)
- 1 cup almond milk (or any preferred milk alternative)
- 1/4 cup honey or maple syrup (for a vegan option)
- 1 teaspoon vanilla extract
- 1/2 teaspoon ground cinnamon
- 1/4 teaspoon ground ginger
- 1/4 teaspoon ground cardamom
- 1/4 teaspoon ground cloves
- Ice cubes
- Cinnamon sticks (for garnish)
- Star anise (for garnish)
- Ground nutmeg (for garnish)

DIRECTIONS

- Brew 2 cups of strong chai tea using chai tea bags or loose-leaf chai tea. Let it cool to room temperature, then chill in the refrigerator
- In a large pitcher, combine the chilled chai tea, almond milk, honey or maple syrup, vanilla extract, ground cinnamon, ground ginger, ground cardamom, and ground cloves
- Stir well to ensure the sweetener and spices are fully dissolved and the flavors are well combined
- Add ice cubes to a cocktail shaker, pour in the chai mixture from the pitcher, and shake vigorously for about 15-20 seconds to combine all ingredients and chill the mixture thoroughly
- Fill four tall glasses with ice cubes
- Strain the mixture equally into the prepared glasses
- For a beautiful presentation, garnish each glass with a cinnamon stick, star anise, and a sprinkle of ground nutmeg

NOTES

Dairy-Free Option: Use any dairy-free milk alternative like almond milk, coconut milk, or oat milk

MULLED BERRY PUNCH

TOTAL TIME	CALORIES	SERVES
20 MINS	90 KCAL	4

DIRECTIONS

- Combine the mixed berries, apple cider, cranberry juice, and fresh orange juice in a medium saucepan
- Bring the mixture to a simmer over medium heat, stirring occasionally
- Once it starts to simmer, add the honey or agave syrup, ground cinnamon, ground nutmeg, ground cloves, and vanilla extract. Stir well until the sweetener and spices are fully dissolved and the flavors are well combined
- Let the mixture simmer for 10 minutes to allow the flavors to meld together
- After simmering, strain the mixture through a fine mesh strainer into a pitcher to remove the berry pulp and spices
- Let the mixture cool to room temperature, then chill it in the refrigerator
- Fill four tall glasses with ice cubes
- Pour the chilled mulled berry mixture equally into the prepared glasses
- Top each glass with sparkling water to add enthusiasm and volume to the mocktail
- For a beautiful presentation, garnish each glass with an orange slice, fresh berries, and a cinnamon stick

INGREDIENTS

- 2 cups mixed berries (fresh or frozen; e.g., strawberries, raspberries, blueberries, blackberries)
- 2 cups apple cider
- 1 cup cranberry juice (unsweetened)
- 1/2 cup fresh orange juice (about 2-3 oranges)
- 1/4 cup honey or agave syrup (for a vegan option)
- 1 teaspoon ground cinnamon
- 1/2 teaspoon ground nutmeg
- 1/2 teaspoon ground cloves
- 1 teaspoon vanilla extract
- 1 cup sparkling water
- Orange slices (for garnish)
- Fresh berries (for garnish)
- Cinnamon sticks (for garnish)

HAZELNUT DELIGHT

TOTAL TIME	CALORIES	SERVES
15 MINS	100 KCAL	4

DIRECTIONS

- In a large pitcher, combine the hazelnut milk, fresh apple cider, fresh orange juice, honey or maple syrup, and vanilla extract
- Stir well to ensure the sweetener is fully dissolved
- Add the ground cinnamon, ground nutmeg, and ground cloves to the mixture
- Stir thoroughly to ensure the spices are evenly distributed
- Add ice cubes to a cocktail shaker, pour in the mixture from the pitcher, and shake vigorously for about 15-20 seconds to combine all ingredients and chill the mixture thoroughly
- Fill four tall glasses with ice cubes
- Strain the mixture equally into the prepared glasses
- Garnish each glass with crushed hazelnuts around the rim, a sprinkle of orange zest, and a cinnamon stick for a beautiful presentation

INGREDIENTS

- 1 cup hazelnut milk (store-bought or homemade)
- 1/2 cup fresh apple cider
- 1/4 cup fresh orange juice (about 1-2 oranges)
- 1/4 cup honey or maple syrup (for a vegan option)
- 1 teaspoon vanilla extract
- 1/2 teaspoon ground cinnamon
- 1/4 teaspoon ground nutmeg
- 1/4 teaspoon ground cloves
- Ice cubes
- Crushed hazelnuts (for garnish)
- Orange zest (for garnish)
- Cinnamon sticks (for garnish)

NOTES

Allergy-Friendly Option: Use a different milk alternative if hazelnut is a concern, such as almond or oat milk. Ensure all ingredients, particularly the sweetener, are free from allergens and cross-contamination warnings on the packaging

APPLE GINGER PUNCH

TOTAL TIME	CALORIES	SERVES
15 MINS	70 KCAL	4

DIRECTIONS

- In a small saucepan, combine the honey or agave syrup with 1/4 cup of water and the freshly grated ginger
- Bring to a simmer over medium heat, stirring occasionally, until the honey is fully dissolved and the mixture is fragrant
- Remove from heat and let it cool slightly, then strain to remove the ginger pieces
- Combine the apple cider, fresh lemon juice, ginger syrup, ground cinnamon, and ground cloves in a large pitcher
- Stir well to ensure the syrup and spices are fully dissolved and the flavors are well combined
- Add ice cubes to a cocktail shaker, pour in the mixture from the pitcher, and shake vigorously for about 15-20 seconds to combine all ingredients and chill the mixture thoroughly
- Fill four tall glasses with ice cubes
- Strain the mixture equally into the prepared glasses
- Top each glass with sparkling water to add enthusiasm and volume to the mocktail
- For a beautiful presentation, garnish each glass with apple slices, lemon slices, and a sprig of fresh mint

INGREDIENTS

- 2 cups apple cider
- 1 cup sparkling water
- 1/2 cup fresh lemon juice (about 4-5 lemons)
- 1/4 cup honey or agave syrup (for a vegan option)
- 2 tablespoons freshly grated ginger
- 1 teaspoon ground cinnamon
- 1/4 teaspoon ground cloves
- Ice cubes
- Apple slices (for garnish)
- Lemon slices (for garnish)
- Fresh mint leaves (for garnish)

CRANBERRY SPRITZ

TOTAL TIME	CALORIES	SERVES
15 MINS	60 KCAL	4

DIRECTIONS

- In a large pitcher, combine the cranberry juice, fresh orange juice, fresh lime juice, and honey or agave syrup
- Stir well to ensure the sweetener is fully dissolved
- Add the ground cinnamon and ground cloves to the juice mixture
- Stir thoroughly to ensure the spices are evenly distributed
- Add ice cubes to a cocktail shaker, pour in the mixture from the pitcher, and shake vigorously for about 15-20 seconds to combine all ingredients and chill the mixture thoroughly
- Fill four tall glasses with ice cubes
- Strain the mixture equally into the prepared glasses
- Top each glass with sparkling water to add enthusiasm and volume to the mocktail
- For a beautiful presentation, garnish each glass with fresh cranberries, orange slices, lime slices, and a sprig of fresh mint

INGREDIENTS

- 2 cups cranberry juice (unsweetened)
- 1 cup sparkling water
- 1/2 cup fresh orange juice (about 2-3 oranges)
- 1/4 cup fresh lime juice (about 3-4 limes)
- 1/4 cup honey or agave syrup (for a vegan option)
- 1/2 teaspoon ground cinnamon
- 1/4 teaspoon ground cloves
- Ice cubes
- Fresh cranberries (for garnish)
- Orange slices (for garnish)
- Lime slices (for garnish)
- Fresh mint leaves (for garnish)

NOTES

- Vitamin C: 25% DV
- Calcium: 2% DV
- Iron: 1% DV

BUTTERNUT SQUASH COOLER

TOTAL TIME	CALORIES	SERVES
20 MINS	80 KCAL	4

DIRECTIONS

- Peel and cube a small butternut squash. Steam or boil until tender
- Blend the cooked squash until smooth. Let it cool before using
- In a large pitcher, combine the butternut squash puree, apple cider, fresh orange juice, honey or maple syrup, ground cinnamon, ground ginger, ground nutmeg, and vanilla extract
- Stir well to ensure the sweetener and spices are fully dissolved and the flavors are well combined
- Add ice cubes to a cocktail shaker, pour in the mixture from the pitcher, and shake vigorously for about 15-20 seconds to combine all ingredients and chill the mixture thoroughly
- Fill four tall glasses with ice cubes
- Strain the mixture equally into the prepared glasses
- Top each glass with sparkling water to add enthusiasm and volume to the mocktail
- Garnish each glass with an orange slice and a sprig of fresh thyme for a beautiful presentation

INGREDIENTS

- 1 cup butternut squash puree (fresh or canned)
- 2 cups apple cider
- 1/2 cup fresh orange juice (about 2-3 oranges)
- 1/4 cup honey or maple syrup (for a vegan option)
- 1 teaspoon ground cinnamon
- 1/2 teaspoon ground ginger
- 1/4 teaspoon ground nutmeg
- 1 teaspoon vanilla extract
- 1 cup sparkling water
- Ice cubes
- Orange slices (for garnish)
- Fresh thyme sprigs (for garnish)

CINNAMON APPLE CHILLER

TOTAL TIME	CALORIES	SERVES
15 MINS	**70 KCAL**	**4**

DIRECTIONS

- In a large pitcher, combine the apple cider, sparkling water, fresh lemon juice, honey or maple syrup, ground cinnamon, ground nutmeg, and vanilla extract
- Stir well to ensure the sweetener and spices are fully dissolved and the flavors are well combined
- Add ice cubes to a cocktail shaker, pour in the mixture from the pitcher, and shake vigorously for about 15-20 seconds to combine all ingredients and chill the mixture thoroughly
- Fill four tall glasses with ice cubes
- Strain the mixture equally into the prepared glasses
- For a beautiful presentation, garnish each glass with apple slices, lemon slices, and a cinnamon stick

INGREDIENTS

- 2 cups apple cider
- 1 cup sparkling water
- 1/2 cup fresh lemon juice (about 4-5 lemons)
- 1/4 cup honey or maple syrup (for a vegan option)
- 2 teaspoons ground cinnamon
- 1 teaspoon ground nutmeg
- 1 teaspoon vanilla extract
- Ice cubes
- Apple slices (for garnish)
- Lemon slices (for garnish)
- Cinnamon sticks (for garnish)

NOTES

- Vitamin C: 30% DV
- Calcium: 2% DV
- Iron: 1% DV

PLUM SPICE FIZZ

TOTAL TIME	CALORIES	SERVES
20 MINS	80 KCAL	4

DIRECTIONS

- Blend the chopped plums in a blender until smooth. Then, strain the plum puree through a fine mesh strainer into a bowl or pitcher to remove any pulp
- In a large pitcher, combine the plum puree, fresh orange juice, fresh lemon juice, honey or agave syrup, ground cinnamon, ground nutmeg, ground cloves, and vanilla extract
- Stir well to ensure the sweetener and spices are fully dissolved and the flavors are well combined
- Add ice cubes to a cocktail shaker, pour in the mixture from the pitcher, and shake vigorously for about 15-20 seconds to combine all ingredients and chill the mixture thoroughly
- Fill four tall glasses with ice cubes
- Strain the mixture equally into the prepared glasses
- Top each glass with sparkling water to add enthusiasm and volume to the mocktail
- For a beautiful presentation, garnish each glass with plum slices, a sprinkle of orange zest, and a sprig of fresh mint

INGREDIENTS

- 4 ripe plums, pitted and chopped
- 2 cups sparkling water
- 1 cup fresh orange juice (about 3-4 oranges)
- 1/4 cup fresh lemon juice (about 2-3 lemons)
- 1/4 cup honey or agave syrup (for a vegan option)
- 1 teaspoon ground cinnamon
- 1/2 teaspoon ground nutmeg
- 1/4 teaspoon ground cloves
- 1 teaspoon vanilla extract
- Ice cubes
- Plum slices (for garnish)
- Orange zest (for garnish)
- Fresh mint leaves (for garnish)

CARROT GINGER SPARKLE

TOTAL TIME	CALORIES	SERVES
15 MINS	70 KCAL	4

INGREDIENTS

- 2 cups fresh carrot juice (about 6-8 carrots)
- 1 cup sparkling water
- 1/2 cup fresh orange juice (about 2-3 oranges)
- 1/4 cup fresh lemon juice (about 2-3 lemons)
- 2 tablespoons freshly grated ginger
- 1/4 cup honey or agave syrup (for a vegan option)
- 1 teaspoon ground cinnamon
- 1/2 teaspoon ground nutmeg
- 1 teaspoon vanilla extract
- Ice cubes
- Carrot ribbons (for garnish)
- Orange slices (for garnish)
- Fresh mint leaves (for garnish)

DIRECTIONS

- If using whole carrots, wash, peel, and juice them using a juicer to obtain 2 cups of fresh carrot juice. If using store-bought carrot juice, ensure it is fresh and without added sugars
- In a large pitcher, combine the fresh carrot juice, fresh orange juice, fresh lemon juice, freshly grated ginger, honey or agave syrup, ground cinnamon, ground nutmeg, and vanilla extract
- Stir well to ensure the sweetener and spices are fully dissolved and the flavors are well combined
- Add ice cubes to a cocktail shaker, pour in the mixture from the pitcher, and shake vigorously for about 15-20 seconds to combine all ingredients and chill the mixture thoroughly
- Fill four tall glasses with ice cubes
- Strain the mixture equally into the prepared glasses
- Top each glass with sparkling water to add enthusiasm and volume to the mocktail
- Garnish each glass with carrot ribbons, orange slices, and a sprig of fresh mint for a beautiful presentation

ROSEMARY MAPLE MOCKTAIL

TOTAL TIME	CALORIES	SERVES
15 MINS	60 KCAL	4

DIRECTIONS

- In a small saucepan, combine the pure maple syrup and one sprig of fresh rosemary
- Heat over low heat for about 5 minutes, stirring occasionally to infuse the rosemary flavor into the syrup
- Remove from heat and let it cool slightly, then remove the rosemary sprig
- In a large pitcher, combine the sparkling water, fresh apple cider, fresh lemon juice, rosemary-infused maple syrup, ground cinnamon, ground nutmeg, and vanilla extract
- Stir well to ensure the syrup and spices are fully dissolved and the flavors are well combined
- Add ice cubes to a cocktail shaker, pour in the mixture from the pitcher, and shake vigorously for about 15-20 seconds to combine all ingredients and chill the mixture thoroughly
- Fill four tall glasses with ice cubes
- Strain the mixture equally into the prepared glasses
- Garnish each glass with a lemon slice and a sprig of fresh rosemary for a beautiful presentation

INGREDIENTS

- 2 cups sparkling water
- 1 cup fresh apple cider
- 1/2 cup fresh lemon juice (about 4-5 lemons)
- 1/4 cup pure maple syrup
- 2 sprigs fresh rosemary
- 1 teaspoon ground cinnamon
- 1/2 teaspoon ground nutmeg
- 1 teaspoon vanilla extract
- Ice cubes
- Lemon slices (for garnish)
- Fresh rosemary sprigs (for garnish)

WINTER WONDERS

PEPPERMINT HOT CHOCOLATE

INGREDIENTS

- 4 cups whole milk (or any preferred milk alternative)
- 1 cup heavy cream (optional for extra creaminess)
- 1/2 cup semi-sweet chocolate chips
- 1/4 cup unsweetened cocoa powder
- 1/4 cup sugar (or to taste)
- 1 teaspoon vanilla extract
- 1/2 teaspoon peppermint extract
- Whipped cream (for garnish)
- Crushed candy canes (for garnish)
- Chocolate shavings (for garnish)
- Peppermint sticks (for garnish)

TOTAL TIME	CALORIES	SERVES
15 MINS	250 KCAL	4

DIRECTIONS

- In a medium saucepan, combine the whole milk and heavy cream
- Heat over medium heat until it begins to steam, but do not let it boil
- Add the semi-sweet chocolate chips and unsweetened cocoa powder to the milk mixture
- Whisk continuously until the chocolate is fully melted and the mixture is smooth
- Add the sugar, vanilla extract, and peppermint extract to the mixture
- Stir well to ensure the sugar is fully dissolved and the flavors are well combined
- For an extra frothy texture, you can carefully transfer the hot chocolate mixture to a blender and blend on high for a few seconds. Be cautious with hot liquids in the blender, ensuring the lid is secure
- Pour the Peppermint Hot Chocolate into four mugs
- Top each mug with a generous dollop of whipped cream
- Sprinkle crushed candy canes and chocolate shavings on top
- Garnish with a peppermint stick for a festive touch

POMEGRANATE SPARKLER

INGREDIENTS

- 2 cups pomegranate juice
- 1 cup sparkling water
- 1/2 cup fresh orange juice (about 2-3 oranges)
- 1/4 cup fresh lime juice (about 2-3 limes)
- 1/4 cup honey or agave syrup (for a vegan option)
- 1 teaspoon vanilla extract
- Pomegranate seeds (for garnish)
- Orange slices (for garnish)
- Fresh mint leaves (for garnish)
- Ice cubes

TOTAL TIME	CALORIES	SERVES
15 MINS	70 KCAL	4

DIRECTIONS

- In a large pitcher, combine the pomegranate juice, fresh orange juice, fresh lime juice, honey or agave syrup, and vanilla extract
- Stir well to ensure the sweetener is fully dissolved and the flavors are well combined
- Add ice cubes to a cocktail shaker, pour in the juice mixture from the pitcher, and shake vigorously for about 15-20 seconds to combine all ingredients and chill the mixture thoroughly
- Fill four tall glasses with ice cubes
- Strain the mixture equally into the prepared glasses
- Top each glass with sparkling water to add enthusiasm and volume to the mocktail
- Garnish each glass with pomegranate seeds, an orange slice, and a sprig of fresh mint for a beautiful presentation

NOTES

Sugar-Free Option: Replace honey or agave syrup with a sugar-free sweetener such as stevia or monk fruit sweetener

CRANBERRY GINGER ALE

TOTAL TIME	CALORIES	SERVES
15 MINS	70 KCAL	4

INGREDIENTS

- 2 cups cranberry juice (unsweetened)
- 1 cup ginger ale
- 1/2 cup fresh orange juice (about 2-3 oranges)
- 1/4 cup fresh lime juice (about 2-3 limes)
- 2 tablespoons freshly grated ginger
- 1/4 cup honey or agave syrup (for a vegan option)
- 1 teaspoon vanilla extract
- Cranberries (for garnish)
- Lime slices (for garnish)
- Fresh mint leaves (for garnish)
- Ice cubes

DIRECTIONS

- In a small saucepan, combine the honey or agave syrup with 1/4 cup of water and the freshly grated ginger
- Bring to a simmer over medium heat, stirring occasionally, until the honey is fully dissolved and the mixture is fragrant
- Remove from heat and let it cool slightly, then strain to remove the ginger pieces
- In a large pitcher, combine the cranberry juice, fresh orange juice, fresh lime juice, and ginger syrup
- Stir well to ensure the syrup is fully dissolved and the flavors are well combined
- Add ice cubes to a cocktail shaker, pour in the juice mixture from the pitcher, and shake vigorously for about 15-20 seconds to combine all ingredients and chill the mixture thoroughly
- Fill four tall glasses with ice cubes
- Strain the mixture equally into the prepared glasses
- Top each glass with ginger ale to add enthusiasm and volume to the mocktail
- For a beautiful presentation, garnish each glass with cranberries, lime slices, and a sprig of fresh mint

EGGNOG MOCKTAIL

TOTAL TIME	CALORIES	SERVES
20 MINS	200 KCAL	4

DIRECTIONS

- Combine the whole milk and heavy cream in a medium saucepan
- Heat over medium heat until it begins to steam, but do not let it boil
- In a large mixing bowl, whisk together the egg yolks and granulated sugar until the mixture is smooth and pale in color
- Gradually add a ladleful of the hot milk mixture to the egg yolk mixture, whisking constantly to temper the eggs
- Slowly pour the tempered egg mixture back into the saucepan with the remaining milk and cream, whisking continuously
- Cook the mixture over medium heat, stirring constantly, until it thickens slightly and coats the back of a spoon (about 5-7 minutes). Do not let it boil
- Remove the saucepan from the heat
- Stir in the vanilla extract, ground cinnamon, ground nutmeg, and ground cloves until well combined
- Pour the eggnog mixture into a pitcher and let it cool to room temperature
- Refrigerate for at least 2 hours or until thoroughly chilled
- Pour the chilled eggnog into four glasses
- Top each glass with a dollop of whipped cream
- Sprinkle with ground nutmeg.
- Garnish with a cinnamon stick for a festive touch

INGREDIENTS

- 2 cups whole milk (or any preferred milk alternative)
- 1 cup heavy cream (optional for extra creaminess)
- 4 large egg yolks
- 1/2 cup granulated sugar
- 1 teaspoon vanilla extract
- 1 teaspoon ground cinnamon
- 1/2 teaspoon ground nutmeg
- 1/4 teaspoon ground cloves
- Whipped cream (for garnish)
- Ground nutmeg (for garnish)
- Cinnamon sticks (for garnish)

SPICED HOT APPLE CIDER

TOTAL TIME	CALORIES	SERVES
20 MINS	100 KCAL	4

INGREDIENTS

- 4 cups apple cider
- 1/4 cup fresh orange juice (about 1-2 oranges)
- 2 tablespoons fresh lemon juice (about 1 lemon)
- 2 tablespoons honey or maple syrup (for a vegan option)
- 2 cinnamon sticks
- 4 whole cloves
- 4 whole allspice berries
- 1-inch piece of fresh ginger, thinly sliced
- 1/4 teaspoon ground nutmeg
- 1 teaspoon vanilla extract
- Orange slices (for garnish)
- Lemon slices (for garnish)
- Cinnamon sticks (for garnish)
- Star anise (for garnish)

DIRECTIONS

- In a large saucepan, combine the apple cider, fresh orange juice, fresh lemon juice, honey or maple syrup, cinnamon sticks, whole cloves, whole allspice berries, and sliced ginger
- Place the saucepan over medium heat and bring the mixture to a gentle simmer
- Reduce the heat to low and let it simmer for 15 minutes, allowing the spices to infuse into the cider
- Stir in the vanilla extract and ground nutmeg
- Continue to simmer for an additional 2 minutes
- Remove the saucepan from the heat
- Carefully strain the hot apple cider into a large pitcher or another clean saucepan to remove the spices and ginger slices
- Pour the hot apple cider into four heatproof glasses or mugs
- For a festive presentation, garnish each glass with an orange slice, a lemon slice, a cinnamon stick, and a star anise

NOTES
- Vitamin C: 15% DV
- Calcium: 2% DV
- Iron: 2% DV

WINTER CITRUS PUNCH

TOTAL TIME	CALORIES	SERVES
15 MINS	80 KCAL	4

DIRECTIONS

- In a large pitcher, combine the fresh orange juice, fresh grapefruit juice, fresh lemon juice, fresh lime juice, and honey or agave syrup
- Stir well to ensure the sweetener is fully dissolved
- Stir in the vanilla extract, ground cinnamon, and ground cloves until well combined
- Add ice cubes to a cocktail shaker, pour in the juice mixture from the pitcher, and shake vigorously for about 15-20 seconds to combine all ingredients and chill the mixture thoroughly
- Fill four tall glasses with ice cubes
- Strain the mixture equally into the prepared glasses
- Top each glass with sparkling water to add effervescence and volume to the mocktail
- Garnish each glass with slices of orange, grapefruit, lemon, and lime
- Add a sprig of fresh mint for a beautiful presentation

INGREDIENTS

- 1 cup fresh orange juice (about 2-3 oranges)
- 1 cup fresh grapefruit juice (about 1-2 grapefruits)
- 1/2 cup fresh lemon juice (about 2-3 lemons)
- 1/2 cup fresh lime juice (about 3-4 limes)
- 1/4 cup honey or agave syrup (for a vegan option)
- 1 cup sparkling water
- 1 teaspoon vanilla extract
- 1/2 teaspoon ground cinnamon
- 1/4 teaspoon ground cloves
- Ice cubes
- Orange slices (for garnish)
- Grapefruit slices (for garnish)
- Lemon slices (for garnish)
- Lime slices (for garnish)
- Fresh mint leaves (for garnish)

NOTES

- Vitamin C: 50% DV
- Calcium: 4% DV
- Iron: 2% DV

CHOCOLATE MINT FIZZ

INGREDIENTS

- 2 cups whole milk (or any preferred milk alternative)
- 1/2 cup heavy cream (optional for extra creaminess)
- 1/2 cup semi-sweet chocolate chips
- 2 tablespoons unsweetened cocoa powder
- 1/4 cup sugar (or to taste)
- 1 teaspoon vanilla extract
- 1/2 teaspoon peppermint extract
- 1 cup sparkling water
- Ice cubes
- Whipped cream (for garnish)
- Chocolate shavings (for garnish)
- Fresh mint leaves (for garnish)
- Crushed candy canes (for garnish)

TOTAL TIME	CALORIES	SERVES
15 MINS	180 KCAL	4

DIRECTIONS

- In a medium saucepan, combine the whole milk and heavy cream
- Heat over medium heat until it begins to steam, but do not let it boil
- Add the semi-sweet chocolate chips and unsweetened cocoa powder to the milk mixture
- Whisk continuously until the chocolate is fully melted and the mixture is smooth
- Add the sugar, vanilla extract, and peppermint extract to the mixture
- Stir well to ensure the sugar is fully dissolved and the flavors are well combined
- Remove the saucepan from the heat and let the mixture cool to room temperature
- Refrigerate for at least 1 hour or until thoroughly chilled
- Fill four tall glasses with ice cubes
- Pour the chilled chocolate mint mixture equally into the prepared glasses
- Top each glass with sparkling water to add enthusiasm and volume to the mocktail
- Garnish each glass with a dollop of whipped cream, chocolate shavings, fresh mint leaves, and a sprinkle of crushed candy canes for a festive touch

VANILLA ALMOND DELIGHT

TOTAL TIME	CALORIES	SERVES
15 MINS	120 KCAL	4

DIRECTIONS

- In a large pitcher, combine the almond milk, coconut milk, and maple syrup or honey
- Stir well to ensure the sweetener is fully dissolved
- Stir in the vanilla extract, almond extract, ground cinnamon, and ground nutmeg until well combined
- Add ice cubes to a cocktail shaker, pour in the milk mixture from the pitcher, and shake vigorously for about 15-20 seconds to combine all ingredients and chill the mixture thoroughly
- Fill four glasses with ice cubes
- Strain the mixture equally into the prepared glasses
- Garnish each glass with a dollop of whipped cream
- Sprinkle with toasted almond slices and a dash of ground cinnamon
- Add a sprig of fresh mint for a beautiful presentation

INGREDIENTS

- 2 cups almond milk (unsweetened)
- 1/2 cup coconut milk (for added creaminess)
- 1/4 cup pure maple syrup or honey (for a vegan option)
- 1 teaspoon vanilla extract
- 1/2 teaspoon almond extract
- 1/2 teaspoon ground cinnamon
- 1/4 teaspoon ground nutmeg
- Ice cubes
- Whipped cream (for garnish)
- Toasted almond slices (for garnish)
- Ground cinnamon (for garnish)
- Fresh mint leaves (for garnish)

NOTES

- Vitamin D: 20% DV
- Calcium: 30% DV
- Iron: 2% DV

MULLED APPLE JUICE

TOTAL TIME	CALORIES	SERVES
20 MINS	90 KCAL	4

INGREDIENTS

- 4 cups apple juice (preferably unsweetened)
- 1/2 cup fresh orange juice (about 2-3 oranges)
- 2 tablespoons fresh lemon juice (about 1 lemon)
- 1/4 cup honey or maple syrup (for a vegan option)
- 2 cinnamon sticks
- 4 whole cloves
- 4 whole allspice berries
- 1 star anise
- 1-inch piece of fresh ginger, sliced
- 1/2 teaspoon ground nutmeg
- 1 teaspoon vanilla extract
- Orange slices (for garnish)
- Lemon slices (for garnish)
- Cinnamon sticks (for garnish)
- Star anise (for garnish)

DIRECTIONS

- In a large saucepan, combine the apple juice, fresh orange juice, fresh lemon juice, honey or maple syrup, cinnamon sticks, whole cloves, whole allspice berries, star anise, and sliced ginger
- Place the saucepan over medium heat and bring the mixture to a gentle simmer
- Reduce the heat to low and let it simmer for 15 minutes, allowing the spices to infuse into the juice
- Stir in the vanilla extract and ground nutmeg
- Continue to simmer for an additional 2 minutes
- Remove the saucepan from the heat
- Carefully strain the hot apple juice into a large pitcher or another clean saucepan to remove the spices and ginger slices
- Pour the mulled apple juice into four heatproof glasses or mugs
- For a festive presentation, garnish each glass with an orange slice, a lemon slice, a cinnamon stick, and a star anise

NOTES

Vitamin C: 20% DV

GINGERBREAD MOCKTAIL

TOTAL TIME	CALORIES	SERVES
15 MINS	150 KCAL	4

DIRECTIONS

- In a large pitcher, combine the almond milk, coconut milk, molasses, and maple syrup or honey
- Stir well to ensure the sweeteners are fully dissolved
- Stir in the vanilla extract, ground ginger, ground cinnamon, ground nutmeg, and ground cloves until well combined
- Add ice cubes to a cocktail shaker, pour in the milk mixture from the pitcher, and shake vigorously for about 15-20 seconds to combine all ingredients and chill the mixture thoroughly
- Fill four glasses with ice cubes
- Strain the mixture equally into the prepared glasses
- Garnish each glass with a dollop of whipped cream
- Sprinkle with crushed gingerbread cookies and a dash of ground cinnamon
- Add a sprig of fresh mint for a beautiful presentation

INGREDIENTS

- 2 cups almond milk (or any preferred milk alternative)
- 1/2 cup coconut milk (for added creaminess)
- 1/4 cup molasses
- 1/4 cup maple syrup or honey (for a vegan option)
- 1 teaspoon vanilla extract
- 1 teaspoon ground ginger
- 1/2 teaspoon ground cinnamon
- 1/4 teaspoon ground nutmeg
- 1/4 teaspoon ground cloves
- Ice cubes
- Whipped cream (for garnish)
- Crushed gingerbread cookies (for garnish)
- Ground cinnamon (for garnish)
- Fresh mint leaves (for garnish)

NOTES

- Vitamin D: 20% DV
- Calcium: 25% DV
- Iron: 2% DV

WINTER BERRY REFRESHER

TOTAL TIME	CALORIES	SERVES
15 MINS	80 KCAL	4

DIRECTIONS

- In a large pitcher, combine the cranberry juice, pomegranate juice, fresh orange juice, fresh lemon juice, and honey or agave syrup
- Stir well to ensure the sweetener is fully dissolved
- Stir in the vanilla extract, ground cinnamon, and ground nutmeg until well combined
- Add ice cubes to a cocktail shaker, pour in the juice mixture from the pitcher, and shake vigorously for about 15-20 seconds to combine all ingredients and chill the mixture thoroughly
- Fill four tall glasses with ice cubes
- Strain the mixture equally into the prepared glasses
- Top each glass with sparkling water to add enthusiasm and volume to the mocktail
- For a beautiful presentation, garnish each glass with fresh cranberries, pomegranate seeds, an orange slice, and a sprig of fresh mint

INGREDIENTS

- 1 cup cranberry juice (unsweetened)
- 1 cup pomegranate juice
- 1/2 cup fresh orange juice (about 2-3 oranges)
- 1/4 cup fresh lemon juice (about 2-3 lemons)
- 1/4 cup honey or agave syrup (for a vegan option)
- 1 cup sparkling water
- 1 teaspoon vanilla extract
- 1/2 teaspoon ground cinnamon
- 1/4 teaspoon ground nutmeg
- Fresh cranberries (for garnish)
- Pomegranate seeds (for garnish)
- Orange slices (for garnish)
- Fresh mint leaves (for garnish)
- Ice cubes

NOTES

- Vitamin C: 30% DV
- Calcium: 2% DV
- Iron: 2% DV

FROSTY PINEAPPLE

INGREDIENTS

- 2 cups fresh pineapple juice
- 1 cup coconut water
- 1/2 cup fresh lime juice (about 4-5 limes)
- 1/4 cup honey or agave syrup (for a vegan option)
- 1 teaspoon vanilla extract
- 1/2 teaspoon ground ginger
- 1/4 teaspoon ground nutmeg
- 1 cup sparkling water
- Ice cubes
- Pineapple slices (for garnish)
- Lime slices (for garnish)
- Fresh mint leaves (for garnish)

TOTAL TIME	CALORIES	SERVES
15 MINS	90 KCAL	4

DIRECTIONS

- In a large pitcher, combine the fresh pineapple juice, coconut water, fresh lime juice, and honey or agave syrup
- Stir well to ensure the sweetener is fully dissolved
- Stir in the vanilla extract, ground ginger, and ground nutmeg until well combined
- Add ice cubes to a cocktail shaker, pour in the juice mixture from the pitcher, and shake vigorously for about 15-20 seconds to combine all ingredients and chill the mixture thoroughly
- Fill four tall glasses with ice cubes
- Strain the mixture equally into the prepared glasses
- Top each glass with sparkling water to add enthusiasm and volume to the mocktail
- For a beautiful presentation, garnish each glass with a pineapple slice, a lime slice, and a sprig of fresh mint

NOTES

- Vitamin C: 40% DV
- Calcium: 2% DV
- Iron: 2% DV

CINNAMON SPICE DELIGHT

TOTAL TIME	CALORIES	SERVES
15 MINS	90 KCAL	4

INGREDIENTS

- 2 cups apple cider
- 1 cup cranberry juice
- 1/2 cup fresh orange juice (about 2-3 oranges)
- 1/4 cup fresh lemon juice (about 2-3 lemons)
- 1/4 cup honey or agave syrup (for a vegan option)
- 1 teaspoon vanilla extract
- 2 cinnamon sticks
- 1/2 teaspoon ground nutmeg
- 1/4 teaspoon ground cloves
- 1/4 teaspoon ground ginger
- 1 cup sparkling water
- Ice cubes
- Orange slices (for garnish)
- Cinnamon sticks (for garnish)
- Fresh cranberries (for garnish)

DIRECTIONS

- Combine apple cider, cranberry juice, fresh orange juice, lemon juice, and honey or agave syrup in a large pitcher
- Stir well to ensure the sweetener is fully dissolved
- Stir in the vanilla extract, ground nutmeg, ground cloves, and ground ginger until well combined
- Add the cinnamon sticks to the mixture and let it sit for about 5 minutes to infuse the flavors
- Add ice cubes to a cocktail shaker and pour the juice mixture from the pitcher (removing the cinnamon sticks). Shake vigorously for 15-20 seconds to combine all ingredients and thoroughly chill the mixture
- Fill four tall glasses with ice cubes
- Strain the mixture equally into the prepared glasses
- Top each glass with sparkling water to add enthusiasm and volume to the mocktail
- For a festive touch, garnish each glass with an orange slice, a fresh cinnamon stick, and a few fresh cranberries

HONEY LEMON COOLER

TOTAL TIME	CALORIES	SERVES
15 MINS	50 KCAL	4

DIRECTIONS

- Combine cold water, fresh lemon juice, and honey in a large pitcher
- Stir well to ensure the honey is fully dissolved
- Stir in the vanilla extract, ground ginger, ground cinnamon, and ground nutmeg until well combined
- Add ice cubes to a cocktail shaker, pour in the lemon mixture from the pitcher, and shake vigorously for about 15-20 seconds to combine all ingredients and chill the mixture thoroughly
- Fill four tall glasses with ice cubes
- Strain the mixture equally into the prepared glasses
- Top each glass with sparkling water to add enthusiasm and volume to the mocktail
- Garnish each glass with a lemon slice and a sprig of fresh mint for a beautiful presentation

INGREDIENTS

- 2 cups cold water
- 1 cup fresh lemon juice (about 6-8 lemons)
- 1/4 cup honey (or agave syrup for a vegan option)
- 1 teaspoon vanilla extract
- 1/2 teaspoon ground ginger
- 1/4 teaspoon ground cinnamon
- 1/4 teaspoon ground nutmeg
- 1 cup sparkling water
- Ice cubes
- Lemon slices (for garnish)
- Fresh mint leaves (for garnish)

NOTES

Sugar-Free Option: Replace honey with a sugar-free sweetener such as stevia or monk fruit sweetener

CRANBERRY VANILLA PUNCH

TOTAL TIME	CALORIES	SERVES
15 MINS	70 KCAL	4

DIRECTIONS

- Combine cranberry juice, fresh orange juice, fresh lime juice, and honey or agave syrup in a large pitcher
- Stir well to ensure the sweetener is fully dissolved
- Stir in the vanilla extract, ground cinnamon, and ground nutmeg until well combined
- Add ice cubes to a cocktail shaker, pour in the juice mixture from the pitcher, and shake vigorously for about 15-20 seconds to combine all ingredients and chill the mixture thoroughly
- Fill four tall glasses with ice cubes
- Strain the mixture equally into the prepared glasses
- Top each glass with sparkling water to add enthusiasm and volume to the mocktail
- Garnish each glass with fresh cranberries, an orange slice, a lime slice, and a sprig of fresh mint for a beautiful presentation

INGREDIENTS

- 2 cups cranberry juice (unsweetened)
- 1 cup sparkling water
- 1/2 cup fresh orange juice (about 2-3 oranges)
- 1/4 cup fresh lime juice (about 2-3 limes)
- 1/4 cup honey or agave syrup (for a vegan option)
- 1 teaspoon vanilla extract
- 1/2 teaspoon ground cinnamon
- 1/4 teaspoon ground nutmeg
- Fresh cranberries (for garnish)
- Orange slices (for garnish)
- Lime slices (for garnish)
- Fresh mint leaves (for garnish)
- Ice cubes

NOTES

- Vitamin C: 20% DV
- Calcium: 2% DV
- Iron: 2% DV

CHOCOLATE CHERRY MOCKTAIL

TOTAL TIME	CALORIES	SERVES
15 MINS	120 KCAL	4

DIRECTIONS

- Combine the cherry juice, almond milk, and coconut milk in a large pitcher. Stir well to ensure the liquids are fully mixed
- Add the dark chocolate syrup, cocoa powder, vanilla extract, and almond extract. Stir until well combined
- Put ice cubes in a cocktail shaker, pour the chocolate cherry mixture from the pitcher, and shake vigorously for about 15-20 seconds to mix and chill the mixture
- Fill four glasses with ice cubes
- Pour the mixture equally into the prepared glasses
- Top each glass with sparkling water to add enthusiasm and volume to the mocktail
- For presentation, garnish each glass with a fresh cherry, dark chocolate shavings, and a sprig of fresh mint

INGREDIENTS

- 2 cups cherry juice (unsweetened)
- 1 cup almond milk (or any preferred milk alternative)
- 1/2 cup coconut milk (for added creaminess)
- 1/4 cup dark chocolate syrup
- 2 tablespoons cocoa powder
- 1 teaspoon vanilla extract
- 1/2 teaspoon almond extract
- 1 cup sparkling water
- Ice cubes
- Fresh cherries (for garnish)
- Dark chocolate shavings (for garnish)
- Fresh mint leaves (for garnish)

NOTES

- Vitamin C: 10% DV
- Calcium: 15% DV
- Iron: 4% DV

ALMOND JOY SMOOTHIE

TOTAL TIME	CALORIES	SERVES
15 MINS	180 KCAL	4

DIRECTIONS

- In a blender, combine the almond milk, coconut milk, plain Greek yogurt, almond butter, unsweetened cocoa powder, honey or agave syrup, vanilla extract, almond extract, and ice cubes
- Blend on high speed until the mixture is smooth and creamy, ensuring that all ingredients are well incorporated and the texture is consistent
- Pour the smoothie equally into four tall glasses
- For a decorative touch, garnish each glass with dark chocolate shavings, toasted coconut flakes, and a whole almond

INGREDIENTS

- 2 cups almond milk (or any preferred milk alternative)
- 1 cup coconut milk
- 1/2 cup plain Greek yogurt (or a dairy-free yogurt alternative)
- 1/4 cup almond butter
- 1/4 cup unsweetened cocoa powder
- 1/4 cup honey or agave syrup (for a vegan option)
- 1 teaspoon vanilla extract
- 1/4 teaspoon almond extract
- 1/2 cup ice cubes
- Dark chocolate shavings (for garnish)
- Toasted coconut flakes (for garnish)
- Whole almonds (for garnish)

NOTES

- Protein: 6g
- Vitamin D: 10% DV
- Calcium: 25% DV
- Iron: 8% DV

PEPPERMINT MOCHA

TOTAL TIME	CALORIES	SERVES
15 MINS	110 KCAL	4

DIRECTIONS

- Combine the cooled brewed coffee, almond milk, and coconut milk in a large pitcher
- Stir well to ensure the liquids are fully mixed
- Stir in the unsweetened cocoa powder, honey or agave syrup, vanilla extract, peppermint extract, ground cinnamon, and ground nutmeg until well combined
- Add ice cubes to a cocktail shaker, pour in the peppermint mocha mixture from the pitcher, and shake vigorously for about 15-20 seconds to combine all ingredients and chill the mixture thoroughly
- Fill four tall glasses with ice cubes
- Strain the mixture equally into the prepared glasses
- Garnish each glass with a dollop of whipped cream
- For a festive touch, sprinkle with crushed candy canes, dark chocolate shavings, and a sprig of fresh mint

INGREDIENTS

- 2 cups strong brewed coffee, cooled
- 1 cup almond milk (or any preferred milk alternative)
- 1/2 cup coconut milk
- 1/4 cup unsweetened cocoa powder
- 1/4 cup honey or agave syrup (for a vegan option)
- 1 teaspoon vanilla extract
- 1/2 teaspoon peppermint extract
- 1/4 teaspoon ground cinnamon
- 1/4 teaspoon ground nutmeg
- Ice cubes
- Whipped cream (for garnish)
- Crushed candy canes (for garnish)
- Dark chocolate shavings (for garnish)
- Fresh mint leaves (for garnish)

NOTES

- Vitamin D: 10% DV
- Calcium: 20% DV
- Iron: 4% DV

HAZELNUT HOT COCOA

TOTAL TIME	CALORIES	SERVES
15 MINS	180 KCAL	4

INGREDIENTS

- 3 cups almond milk (or any preferred milk alternative)
- 1/2 cup coconut milk
- 1/2 cup hazelnut spread (such as Nutella, or a dairy-free alternative)
- 1/4 cup unsweetened cocoa powder
- 2 tablespoons honey or agave syrup (for a vegan option)
- 1 teaspoon vanilla extract
- 1/2 teaspoon ground cinnamon
- 1/4 teaspoon ground nutmeg
- 1/4 teaspoon ground cloves
- Whipped cream (for garnish)
- Crushed hazelnuts (for garnish)
- Dark chocolate shavings (for garnish)
- Cinnamon sticks (for garnish)

DIRECTIONS

- In a medium saucepan, combine the almond milk, coconut milk, and hazelnut spread
- Heat over medium heat, stirring constantly, until the hazelnut spread is fully melted and the mixture is smooth
- Stir in the unsweetened cocoa powder and honey or agave syrup until fully combined
- Stir in the vanilla extract, ground cinnamon, ground nutmeg, and ground cloves
- Continue to heat, stirring occasionally, until the mixture is hot but not boiling
- For a frothier texture, use an immersion blender to blend the mixture for 1-2 minutes until frothy and smooth
- Pour the hot cocoa equally into four mugs
- Garnish each mug with a dollop of whipped cream
- Sprinkle with crushed hazelnuts and dark chocolate shavings
- Add a cinnamon stick for a festive touch

VANILLA MAPLE FIZZ

INGREDIENTS

- 2 cups almond milk (or any preferred milk alternative)
- 1/2 cup coconut milk
- 1/4 cup pure maple syrup
- 1 teaspoon vanilla extract
- 1/2 teaspoon ground cinnamon
- 1/4 teaspoon ground nutmeg
- 1 cup sparkling water
- Ice cubes
- Whipped cream (for garnish)
- Crushed pecans (for garnish)
- Cinnamon sticks (for garnish)

TOTAL TIME	CALORIES	SERVES
15 MINS	140 KCAL	4

DIRECTIONS

- Combine the almond milk, coconut milk, and pure maple syrup in a large pitcher
- Stir well to ensure the syrup is fully dissolved
- Stir in the vanilla extract, ground cinnamon, and ground nutmeg until well combined
- Add ice cubes to a cocktail shaker, pour in the vanilla maple mixture from the pitcher, and shake vigorously for about 15-20 seconds to combine all ingredients and chill the mixture thoroughly
- Fill four tall glasses with ice cubes
- Strain the mixture equally into the prepared glasses
- Top each glass with sparkling water to add enthusiasm and volume to the mocktail
- Garnish each glass with a dollop of whipped cream
- Sprinkle with crushed pecans and add a cinnamon stick for a festive touch

NOTES
- Vitamin D: 15% DV
- Calcium: 20% DV
- Iron: 3% DV

HOLIDAY CHEER

TOTAL TIME	CALORIES	SERVES
15 MINS	70 KCAL	4

INGREDIENTS

- 2 cups cranberry juice (unsweetened)
- 1 cup pomegranate juice
- 1/2 cup fresh orange juice (about 2-3 oranges)
- 1/4 cup fresh lime juice (about 2-3 limes)
- 1/4 cup honey or agave syrup (for a vegan option)
- 1 teaspoon vanilla extract
- 1/2 teaspoon ground cinnamon
- 1/4 teaspoon ground nutmeg
- 1/4 teaspoon ground cloves
- 1 cup sparkling water
- Ice cubes
- Fresh cranberries (for garnish)
- Pomegranate seeds (for garnish)
- Orange slices (for garnish)
- Fresh mint leaves (for garnish)

DIRECTIONS

- In a large pitcher, combine the cranberry juice, pomegranate juice, fresh orange juice, fresh lime juice, and honey or agave syrup
- Stir well to ensure the sweetener is fully dissolved
- Stir in the vanilla extract, ground cinnamon, ground nutmeg, and ground cloves until well combined
- Add ice cubes to a cocktail shaker, pour in the juice mixture from the pitcher, and shake vigorously for about 15-20 seconds to combine all ingredients and chill the mixture thoroughly
- Fill four tall glasses with ice cubes
- Strain the mixture equally into the prepared glasses
- Top each glass with sparkling water to add enthusiasm and volume to the mocktail
- Garnish each glass with fresh cranberries, pomegranate seeds, an orange slice, and a sprig of fresh mint for a festive touch

NOTES
- Vitamin C: 20% DV
- Calcium: 2% DV
- Iron: 2% DV

SPICED CITRUS PUNCH

TOTAL TIME	CALORIES	SERVES
15 MINS	**80 KCAL**	**4**

DIRECTIONS

- In a large pitcher, combine the orange juice, grapefruit juice, lemon juice, cranberry juice, and honey or agave syrup
- Stir well to ensure the sweetener is fully dissolved
- Stir in the vanilla extract, ground cinnamon, ground nutmeg, ground cloves, and ground ginger until well combined
- Add ice cubes to a cocktail shaker, pour in the juice mixture from the pitcher, and shake vigorously for about 15-20 seconds to combine all ingredients and chill the mixture thoroughly
- Fill four tall glasses with ice cubes
- Strain the mixture equally into the prepared glasses
- Top each glass with sparkling water to add enthusiasm and volume to the mocktail
- Garnish each glass with an orange slice, a lemon slice, fresh cranberries, and a sprig of fresh mint for a festive touch

INGREDIENTS

- 1 cup orange juice (freshly squeezed)
- 1 cup grapefruit juice (freshly squeezed)
- 1/2 cup lemon juice (freshly squeezed)
- 1/2 cup cranberry juice (unsweetened)
- 1/4 cup honey or agave syrup (for a vegan option)
- 1 teaspoon vanilla extract
- 1/2 teaspoon ground cinnamon
- 1/4 teaspoon ground nutmeg
- 1/4 teaspoon ground cloves
- 1/4 teaspoon ground ginger
- 1 cup sparkling water
- Ice cubes
- Orange slices (for garnish)
- Lemon slices (for garnish)
- Fresh cranberries (for garnish)
- Fresh mint leaves (for garnish)

NOTES

- Vitamin C: 60% DV
- Calcium: 4% DV

SEE YOU

Made in the USA
Monee, IL
12 October 2024

67767604R00057